C000295586

TRADITIONAL
KARATE

TRADITIONAL *K*ARATE

TICKY DONOVAN

An official book of the
Martial Arts Commission

PELHAM BOOKS

Stephen Greene Press

Acknowledgements

I acknowledge with thanks the help I received in the writing of this book from: David Mitchell, who helped me prepare the text and arrange the photographs; Steve Quinn and Simon Kidd who assisted me in demonstrating the techniques.

PELHAM BOOKS
Stephen Greene Press

Published by the Penguin Group
27 Wrights Lane, London W8 5TZ, England
Viking Penguin Inc., 40 West 23rd Street, New York, New York 10010, USA
Stephen Greene Press, 15 Muzzey Street, Lexington, Massachusetts 02173, USA
Penguin Books Australia Ltd, Ringwood, Victoria, Australia
Penguin Books Canada Ltd, 2801 John Street, Markham, Ontario, Canada L3R 1B4
Penguin Books (NZ) Ltd, 182–190 Wairau Road, Auckland 10, New Zealand

Penguin Books Ltd, Registered Offices: Harmondsworth, Middlesex, England

First Published 1989

Typeset in 11 on 12½ Linotron Palatino by Wilmaset, Birkenhead, Wirral
Made and printed in Great Britain by
Butler & Tanner Ltd, Frome, Somerset

ISBN 0 7207 1827 9

A CIP catalogue record for this book is available from the British Library

The Martial Arts are potentially dangerous: the author, producers and publishers will accept no liability for damage or injuries resulting from the performance of techniques described in this book.

Contents

Fred Kidd, 3rd dan, with Simon Kidd, 3rd dan, on his left, and Aden Kidd, 1st dan, on his right

Dedication

I would like to dedicate this book to the memory of the late Fred Kidd. Whenever I think of the things karate stands for, my thoughts always turn to Fred. Fred trained with me for many years and became not only a loyal and respected student, but also a close friend.

Foreword by David Mitchell

I have known David 'Ticky' Donovan for around twenty years. During this time, I have seen him change from being one of our cleverest and most tactical competitors to a national coach without equal anywhere in the world of karate. This changeover has not been made at the expense of his practical ability, because only a few years ago I saw him effortlessly taking one of our European gold medallist men down a peg or two during a squad session.

Ticky is a natural karateka, in the same way that some people are natural pianists, or natural computer whizzes. However, unlike most truly gifted people, he is aware of what it is he is doing right. This means he can pass it on to those of us who are less gifted.

To people like me, who periodically (and quite wrongly) get the feeling that we know it all, a training session with Ticky is a shot in the arm for flagging enthusiasm. I don't care how long you've been training, Ticky has something of interest for you!

Many people think of Ticky simply as a competition coach. Nothing could be further from the truth. Ticky is a traditionalist and through his adherence to the principles of basic karate practice, his karateka have gained worldwide prominence.

So far as I am concerned, the luckiest karateka today are those who train under Ticky Donovan!

February 1988

David Mitchell
Secretary of the British Karate Federation
Chairman of the English Karate Council
Directing Committee member of the European Karate Union
Directing Committee member of the World Union of Karatedo Organisations

Introduction

I used to box when I was younger, and I can remember seeing the first articles about karate when they appeared in the newspapers. This was in the mid-1960s. I remember thinking how interesting the kicking techniques looked, so I decided to find out more. As it happens, I really enjoyed my early karate training in south-west London with Tatsuo Suzuki (8th dan) and Masafumi Shiomitsu (6th dan). After training hard, I eventually received my first dan black belt.

About that time, there was a disagreement within my karate association and the Japanese instructors left. This put me in a difficult position because I wanted more training. I took up the style of shotokan karate as taught by Hirokazu Kanazawa and trained with him until he left Britain. I continued in shotokan for a while with Keinosuke Enoeda (8th dan). Mr. Enoeda is a well respected teacher who was called upon more than once, to coach the British Karate Squad. I next trained with Steve Arneil in the kyokushinkai style of

(left) Ticky with Tatuso Suzuki (*The John Smith Press Agency*) and with (right) Masafumi Shiomitsu

karate, and after some pretty intensive work, I received my black belt in that style.

I also trained with the French instructor, Dominic Valera. Dominic has had a major effect upon my training and I regard him as one of the most talented karateka I have ever met. I have also looked at other martial arts and I am not ashamed to admit that I have learned from these too.

All in all, I've had a pretty mixed training history but at least it has given me a wide appreciation of karate practice and an open-minded approach. There is no 'best' style of karate, and that is a fact!

Karate has many different aspects to it, and it is important to train equally in all of them. Like most young karateka, I was always keen on free sparring and competition. Surprisingly though, whilst sparring attracts a lot of public attention, relatively few karateka actually compete.

Kata training, though interesting, did not seem so exciting as sparring. I know that many karateka actually gave up practising kata, though most of them have now returned to it.

Kata has come to mean many different things to me. For example, it is a good way to train for endurance. Unlike running, kata uses actual karate techniques, so the endurance which it produces is of exactly the right kind. I have also found that kata training improves skill and coordination.

Basic training is the foundation of good karate. Without it, you can do nothing. Basic training teaches you the tools of karate – the techniques themselves. Once you know the techniques, you can begin learning karate. I say this because karate is so much more than just techniques. It is both an art and a discipline. By far the majority of karateka are happiest when training in the techniques of traditional karate and it is that sure knowledge which has prompted me to write this book.

Although I am perhaps best known for my teams' successes in Europe and the world, I am, and always have been, a traditional karateka.

Ticky with Keinosuke Enoeda
(*The John Smith Press Agency*)

Ticky with Dominic Valera

Ticky with Steve Arneil

   Therefore join me in this celebration of traditional karate, to see
whether it has something of value to you. I know that I am still
learning.

David 'Ticky' Donovan, 7th Dan
British and English National Coach
East Ham, London

February 1988

A Short History of Karate

INTRODUCTION

I am a practising karateka, not a historian. For that reason, I don't propose to go into detail about karate's development – that is better left to other less practical books.

Karate is a fighting system which uses the hands and feet to deliver blows, kicks and strikes with great power. The name *karate* means 'empty hand', a phrase which tries to express the idea that karate needs neither external weapons nor thoughts of violence. Sometimes the name *karate-do* is encountered. This means 'the way of karate' and is a method of teaching karate designed to develop the mind as well as the body. *Karate-jutsu* simply means 'karate techniques'.

Originally, karate practice consisted simply of learning techniques, but when the art was introduced into Japan, the Japanese traditions of martial art practice were incorporated into karate training. These taught that learning techniques was only the beginning. Once you had learned them, you trained to develop the art of using them properly.

Throughout this book, I have used only the name *karate*.

KARATE IN OKINAWA

Karate began in the island of Okinawa. This early karate consisted of three principal styles. The Okinawan captial of Shuri gave rise to the *shuri-te* style. The neighbouring city of Naha produced *naha-te*, and a city named Tomari originated *tomari-te*. The word *te* means 'hand'.

Although the three cities were close together, the karate styles they produced were quite separate. Shuri-te used straight-line movements and direct techniques, naha-te used more circular movements, and tomari-te blended the two together.

At first, the practice of karate was forbidden by the authorities but it went on nevertheless, in conditions of great secrecy. Later it came to be taught openly, and was even introduced into schools. Okinawa's Japanese overlords were impressed by karate and asked the

Okinawans to arrange a number of demonstrations. This they did, using a schoolteacher named Gichin Funakoshi.

Funakoshi had studied under two different karate instructors and was a talented karateka. He successfully promoted karate in Okinawa, and eventually moved to the Japanese mainland, where a permanent training centre was set up. This became known as 'The Shotokan'. The style of karate he taught there was also referred to as *Shotokan*.

KARATE IN JAPAN

Funakoshi taught a number of students, some of whom set up their own karate styles. Other Okinawan teachers came to Japan and established their styles too, so by the mid-1930s, quite a few clubs were in existence. Although there are now many different styles of karate, the following are perhaps the best known:

(a) SHOTOKAN: This is the style established by the Okinawan, Gichin Funakoshi. It is based on the teachings of shuri-te, though it has now developed beyond them. It is a powerful style with a large following throughout the world.

(b) WADO RYU: This is the style established by Funakoshi's senior student, the late Hironori Ohtsuka. It uses many evasion techniques and generates power with snapping movements of the joints.

(c) SHITO RYU: This is the style originated by an Okinawan contemporary of Funakoshi, named Kenwa Mabuni. It uses both straight-line and ciruclar movements. Its training syllabus contains the largest number of katas of any style.

(d) SHUKOKAI: This was developed from Mabuni's shito ryu by his senior student, Chojiro Tani. It contains many interesting ideas about power development.

(e) SHOTOKAI: This was founded by Funakoshi's senior student Shigeru Egami. It is similar to the earlier forms of shotokan practice, and is unusual amongst karate styles in that it stresses a 'soft' approach to power generation.

(f) GOJU RYU: This was established by the Okinawan master Chojun Miyagi. He was a contemporary of both Funakoshi and Mabuni. His style is obviously based upon the circular movements of naha-te. Goju ryu uses special training exercises to build strength.

(g) GOJU KAI: This was founded by Miyagi's senior Japanese student, Gogen ('The Cat') Yamaguchi. It is based upon the earlier training methods of goju ryu.

(h) KYOKUSHINKAI: This style is founded by the Korean master Masutatsu Oyama. It has developed from shotokan and goju kai roots, to an original and powerful style of karate, using both direct and circular techniques. Kyokushinkai uses its own form of free-sparring.

(i) SANKUKAI: This style was founded by Yoshinao Nanbu, who previously studied shukokai style. It uses cirular movements and it has a completely original set of katas.

(j) ISHIN RYU : This is the style which I have founded. It is based upon my training in shotokan, wado ryu and kyokushinkai.

Karate spread from Japan, to all the countries of the world and its international development is now in the hands of the World Union of Karatedo Organisations which is recognised by the International Olympic Committee.

It was the WUKO which awarded me a 7th dan, after the team I coached won the world championships team event for the second year in a row. Since that time, I have coached the British team to a third consecutive gold medal.

On a national level, karate styles are practised in clubs. Clubs which practise the same style, or which practise under the same instructors, join together to form associations. In many countries, these associations have themselves joined together to form governing bodies. These then organise national championships and select teams to go to international tournaments.

Training in Karate

Finding a Good Club

To begin your training in karate, you will need to find a good local club. This is not quite as easy as it sounds. There are many karate clubs around, especially in the cities, but not all of them practise to a good standard. Since there are no actual laws to govern karate, anyone can go to a shop, buy a black belt, and open a karate club!

Some students begin training, receive their black belts, and leave to set up their own schools. If these students are not very advanced, or haven't been practising for long, then the standard of their karate will not be as good as it should be.

The best advice I can offer is to look at all of the clubs in your area. Most club coaches will let you watch a training session and if they don't, then delete that particular club from your list. Watch the whole session and if necessary, visit the club on different nights. If the club has been going for a few years, then expect to see several students wearing brown and black belts. Any club that doesn't have senior students training has either not been open long, or it is not a good club and members tend to leave before they make progress.

Ask whether the fee you are charged to join the club includes a personal accident insurance policy. Most good clubs now offer this to members. The typical policy pays a lump sum, or weekly benefit if you are unable to work (or study) following a karate injury. Perhaps more importantly, the policy protects you against the possiblity of a legal action should you injure someone during training.

The Training Uniform

Students of karate, or *karateka* as they are correctly called, all wear a white training uniform. This is known as a *karategi*. It is possible to begin training wearing a tracksuit, but as soon as possible you should buy yourself a karategi. Everyone looks the same in a karategi, so there is no chance for a student to spend extra and look better than another with less money.

Karategis are made from polycotton, or from heavy canvas duck. The former is cheaper and more comfortable to wear. The latter lasts longer but is more expensive to buy. The best place to buy them from is your own club. Whichever you choose, get one that is slightly oversize because all karategis shrink with regular and thorough washing. Each is sold with a white belt, so check the grading syllabus of your association to ensure that this is the correct colour to start with.

Keep your karategi clean and in good repair. A well turned out appearance shows a correct attitude to training. A dirty and ripped karategi indicates a lax attitude.

It's a very good idea to buy a tracksuit as well. Change from your everyday clothes into the karategi and then slip a tracksuit over it. Tracksuits are excellent for keeping warm during lulls in training. However, before you go out and buy an expensive item, check with the club to see whether they use a standard design.

'Flip-flop' sandals (the Japanese call them *zori*) keep your feet clean between the training hall and the changing room. Remove them before you step on to the training surface.

Ask your club coach about fist and shin/instep protectors. These are padded sleeves which protect the arms and legs against those accidental (and painful) clashes which occur from time to time during training.

GRADINGS

Karate uses an assessment method known as 'grading examinations'. These show students how they are improving. Each examination sets a target which is well within the reach of the student. This is very important. Compare it with asking a karateka to win the next national championships. That is obviously not under his control!

Each grade in karate practice is indicated by the wearing of a different coloured belt, the highest grade being that of the black belt. Coloured belt stages are known as *kyu* grades, and each belt has its own set number of techniques to practise. The higher the grade, the better the performance must be. The student must reach the required standard to pass from one grade to the next higher one.

Typically, kyu gradings are held every three to six months, assuming that you have trained regularly for two or three sessions a week. In my own school of ishin ryu, we use the following belt colours:

Red belt   : 6th kyu novice grade
Yellow belt : 5th kyu
Orange belt : 4th kyu
Green belt : 3rd kyu
Blue belt   : 2nd kyu
Brown belt : 1st kyu
Black belt   : 1st dan

Other schools may use different colours and can have up to nine kyu grades.

There are also levels within the black belt known as *dan grades*. Sometimes these are shown as red or yellow stripes on the black belt.

REGULAR TRAINING

Regular training is essential if you want to earn a black belt within a reasonable time. Typically you should allow for two evening sessions per week, plus the occasional weekend course. Each session lasts between ninety minutes and two hours. Some homework is necessary too! If you want to improve quickly, then be prepared to spend an hour each day practising at home.

If someone were to ask me the most common reason for failing to pass a grading examination, I would say it was irregular and infrequent training. Avoid this by keeping a record of your training sessions.

CORRECT BEHAVIOUR

It is said that 'Karate training begins and ends with courtesy.' I believe this.

The training hall is known by the Japanese as the *dojo*. This means 'place of training in the way'. Pause as you enter it and stand upright, with heels together and hands extended flat against the front of your thighs. Lean your head and upper body forwards in a standing bow, making the movement smooth and unhurried (fig. 1). Pause at the lowest point before returning to an upright stance, then go into the training hall. Do the same on leaving it.

Make the bow in the direction of any senior grades who happen to be already present. If the dojo is empty, face the centre of the training hall to bow.

Make the same bow if you are going to train with a partner. Bow at the beginning, and at the end of such training – but not between individual performances.

Perform a formal, kneeling bow at the beginning and end of training. To do this, stand with heels together and arms flat against thighs.

The coach will have designated a student to call out the commands for bringing the class into order. When you hear *seiza!*, squat down with knees open (fig. 2), lower your weight onto your right knee (fig. 3). Bring the left knee down to it and kneel with back straight (fig. 4). On the second command *sensei-ni rei!*, slide your hands forward and off the front of your knees. Lean your body forwards but keep looking towards the instructor (fig. 5). The movement should be smooth and unhurried. Return to a position with your back straight once more.

This is how you show respect for your teacher. Follow it with a

second bow to the senior students. The command for this is *sempai-ni rei*! The coach then rises to his feet. At the final command *kiritsu*, the class rises smoothly together in the reverse action to that used in kneeling.

If the teacher, or a senior grade tells you to sit down, then move back to the wall and sit in a kneeling position or cross-legged. Don't let your feet splay out, where they can trip other students. Don't lounge or lay about. These are the bad habits of a poor karateka.

TYPES OF TRAINING

Karate training can be divided into a number of different topics. These are:

(a) stances

(b) punches and strikes

(c) blocks

(d) kicks

(e) kata

(f) sparring

(g) combinations

(a) Stances

Stances are the postures the body takes up when performing karate techniques. They are the base upon which all karate techniques are built, giving power to punches, resilience to blocks, balance to kicks and the ability to move about freely during sparring.

You must learn not only to settle into a stance without conscious thought, but also to move quickly between stances. Adjustment of stance allows you to set precisely the distance between yourself and your opponent, so your techniques have the best possible chance of success. You must be able to turn about suddenly and with poise, so you can meet an attack from any angle or direction.

(b) Punches and Strikes

Punches and strikes are the hand techniques of karate. By correctly concentrating your force, the hands and arms can be turned into powerful weapons. Karate techniques deliver their power through a small area of impact, so maximum effect is obtained. When this force is applied to the opponent's vulnerable areas, the result is often quite dramatic!

Hand techniques use the closed hand, or fist, and the open hand.

(c) Blocks

Blocks are techniques which prevent an opponent's attack from succeeding. Typically they interrupt his attack, so either it doesn't develop fully, or it is re-directed slightly. Sophisticated blocks use the opponent's own energy against him; they meet his attack and harmonise with it, guiding it smoothly away from vulnerable targets. Typically, blocks are made with the arms, though skilled karateka also use their legs and feet.

(d) Kicks

Because the leg is larger than the arm, it follows that kicks are more powerful though they are also slower. Both of these factors must be considered when deciding how to respond to an attack.

Kicks can reach further than hand techniques, so typically they should be used from greater distances.

(e) Kata

Kata is a form of training in which a whole series of techniques are linked together. I cannot overstress the importance of kata training in achieving a good standard of karate. Regularly practising sequences of techniques, rather than single ones, builds up a fluidity of movement and teaches the linking of techniques.

Kata training can be strenuous, I believe it is a very good way of building the right kind of endurance for karate.

(f) Sparring

Kumite is sparring in all of its various forms. In the most basic form, both attacker and defender know beforehand which of them is going to attack, and with what technique. This type of training teaches the idea of distance and timing, both of which are essential to the higher forms of sparring.

More advanced kumite allows the defender to use any response to a pre-set attack. In free sparring (*jiu kumite*), both attack and response are left to each karateka. As you might imagine, this needs a lot of skill, and knowledge of techniques. For this reason, it is not introduced until later in the training syllabus.

(g) Combinations

Combinations, like kata, are series of basic techniques joined together in such a way as to teach the karateka fluidity. They contain less techniques than kata, however, but use a wider variety of technique.

Preparing to Train

During karate training, you will move your arms and legs in a different way, and in a different rhythm to that which you are accustomed during the day. If you plunge straight into training, your body will take a little while to adjust, and during this time injuries may occur. For this reason I always recommend a good warm up before training proper begins.

A warm up prepares your body to do its best during training, whilst lessening the risk of injury. By using specially selected exercises, the muscles and joints of the body are worked in such a way that muscle action becomes freer and joints more flexible – so when you're reaching for that extra inch of height in your side-kick, you won't harm yourself.

As you increase the pace of the warm up, your heart rate speeds up too, increasing the supply of blood to working muscles. This is much better than a sudden change in pace which would happen if you immediately plunged into hard training. If your training session lasts ninety minutes, then a ten-minute warm up will suffice. You can even use the first techniques of training to complete the warm up, if you want to. Just do them with less than full power and gradually turn on more effort as your arms and legs come to feel looser.

Don't just stop abruptly after training! Your muscles will have been pumping away and will be full of fluids and waste products. If you don't slow down gradually, these will remain in the muscles and cause aches and pains. Continue performing techniques for a short while after training finishes, then run through a short programme of gentle muscle–contracting and stretching exercises. This is known as the 'cool down'.

Mental Warm Up and Cool Down

Warm up is not just physical activity, it involves mental preparation too. People coming into the dojo must change their behaviour to suit the rules of training. How they act in the street may not be appropriate for the karate dojo, and vice versa of course.

Warm up exercises concentrate the mind on the training ahead, so unnecessary worries and distractions are set aside. Certain routines can help the body locate the position of the arms and legs with accuracy, and this is of great importance in the practice of kata. If I ask new students to take up a certain stance, the chances are that they will not get it exactly right simply because they are unaware that their arms and legs are in the wrong places.

Some schools of karate teach seated meditation, or *mokuso* as it is called. Typically this occurs at the very beginning of the session, during the kneeling stage and before training proper begins. Mokuso may also be repeated at the end of training.

BODY PREPARATION

The warm up is intended to bring the body quickly and effectively into a condition where it can work as efficiently and safely as possible. Body preparation is slightly different in that it trains the body to cope with the actual requirements of karate practice.

Karate is like any other physical activity in that it places certain and specialised demands upon the body's systems. If the body is not equal to these demands, then technique quality and/or training intensity suffers.

It may be that I want a student to perform a high kick, but because he has insufficient flexibility in his hip joint he won't be able to carry out the technique properly and so will have to 'cheat'. I might want to train students intensively, but find that some are unable to last the pace and cannot perform powerful and effective techniques over a long enough period. Therefore I must know how to change an individual's physical fitness standard to suit karate practice.

As you proceed through the training programme from grade to grade, you will gradually find yourself acquiring the necessary flexibility and power etc. This is because the programme is designed to present you with a constant but not unattainable challenge.

EXERCISES TO USE

Here is a selection of my favourite exercises, which I have found to be effective over the years. This is not meant to be either a total, or an exclusive list, and you may well come across good additional exercises. If you do so, use them.

Many of the exercises given here may be practised alone, but I have also included a few which require a partner. Exercise at a steady rate and don't just do them on training nights. Train also at home.

Like all coaches, I do a general warm up first, starting at the neck and working down through the body to the ankles. By the time I've finished, every one of my joints will have been worked.

Whole body warm up exercises

I use these to begin the warm up. Start off gently and gradually build up speed, but don't overdo things! The object is to warm yourself up, not tire yourself out before training starts.

Run on the spot, bringing your knees high and pumping your arms. Practise skipping without using a rope and kick your heels up. Jump up and down, making each tenth jump higher than the rest. Spin around in mid-air as you jump, measuring off quarter and half turns accurately. This is a good exercise for learning how to position yourself; it is especially useful for such techniques as spinning reverse roundhouse kick.

General flexibility exercises

Begin by turning your head from side to side (fig 6). Perform this action smoothly and don't force your head to turn too far. Then tilt your head back and look up (fig 7), pause there, and lower it smoothly onto your chest.

6

Lean forwards and flail your arms backwards and forwards (figs. 8 and 9). Keep your arms relaxed and allow them to bend naturally at the elbows. Speed up slowly but still keep your arms relaxed.

When you have been doing this for thirty seconds or so, work on shoulder flexibility by bending your elbow and raising your arm to the side of your head. Take your elbow in your other hand and smoothly draw it back (fig 10). Repeat this a number of times and then change arms. Don't force the joint. If you feel mild discomfort, then stop because that is sufficient.

Move your arm through its full range of movement, extending the elbow fully as you do so (fig. 11). This movement is smooth and unhurried. Repeat it with the other arm. Some people move both arms together, and occasionally they circle them in opposite directions.

Open your legs and bend your knees, so there is no strain on the

7

8

9

10

hamstrings. Then lean forwards as far as you can, raising your arms behind you (figs. 12 and 13).

Work your wrists joints through their full range of movement (fig. 14).

Few people have enough hip flexibility to cope with the demands of karate training. These exercises will help provide it.

Extend one leg and lower your bodyweight over the other (fig. 15). Keep both feet flat on the floor and brace your upper body with your arms. Increase the stretch on your inner thigh by bending your supporting knee still further, but do not bounce on the extended limb. 'Bouncing' will not increase flexibility and may actually cause damage. Repeat this exercise on both sides.

Straighten up from the last exercise and turn your hips so they face in the direction of your leading leg. Lower your weight over your front knee whilst allowing the heel of your rear foot to rise. Keep

15

16

17

18

19

20

your rear knee as straight as possible (fig. 16). Rotate your hips fully so you stretch the muscles on the front and inside of your extended leg.

Turn your hips back and sink down still lower on the supporting leg but allow your extended foot to rise, so only the heel of that foot remains in contact with the floor (fig. 17). Lean forwards to maintain your balance and as before, do not bounce.

Lean your upper body as far forwards as it will go. Rest your hands against the floor (fig. 18). Let your head fall forwards.

Still maintaining this position, lean your upper body forwards and support it with both hands against your leading knee. Keep your body braced but fully straighten your knee. This works on the lower back and on the hamstrings. Increase the stretch by leaning still further forwards (fig. 19).

Stand facing a wall and take up a forward stance. Reach forwards

with both arms to push against the wall and keep both feet flat on the floor (fig 20). Don't bend your back knee.

Stand sideways-on to a wall or support and raise one knee to the side (fig. 21). Bend your knee and take hold of it with your hand. If necessary, use your other hand to keep balance. Pull your knee as high as it will go and hold it there before lowering it. Exercise equally on both legs. This exercise is particularly useful for developing the flexibility needed for a good roundhouse kick.

Bend your knees, placing your palms flat on the floor (fig. 22). Smoothly straighten your knees whilst keeping your palms pressed down (fig. 23). This increases flexibility in the lower back and stretches the hamstrings.

Sit down and extend one leg. Draw the other up to the inside of your thigh (fig. 24). Smoothly lower your head forwards until your forehead touches the extended knee (fig. 25). Hold this lowest position for around ten seconds before returning to an upright position.

Whilst in this sitting position, draw your left foot back against your forehead (fig. 26). Apply force smoothly and do not jerk the foot, especially during the final few inches.

Move forwards onto your hands, as though beginning the press-ups exercise. Drop your knees down to the floor and open them as wide as you can. Shift your weight forwards over your forearms (fig. 27). This stretches the muscles on the insides of the thighs but puts no lateral pressure on the knee joints – a good thing if you have a knee problem. It is also a good exercise for developing the kind of flexibility needed in high roundhouse kicks.

Roll onto your back, and lift your feet over your head. Brace yourself with outstretched arms. Keep your knees straight, supporting yourself on your shoulders and balls of feet (fig. 28).

26

28

29

32

33

34

Reach through with your hands and open your legs out (fig. 29). Roll back slightly onto your lower back and pull your [legs?] forwards and outwards (fig. 30). Do not bend your knees.

The 'splits' is quite a good exercise for stretching leg muscles. Begin with the standard exercise, turning your hips in one direction and extending your legs in front and behind (fig. 31). Whatever you do – don't bounce. Then turn your hips forwards and perform box splits (fig. 32).

Work your hips by standing with heels close together. Sink down and let your heels rise off the floor (fig. 33). Bring your knees together and straighten them, rocking back on your heels as you do so (fig. 34). Rotate your hips by placing your hands upon your knees and circling them (figs. 35 and 36).

Complete basic exercises by circling your ankles (fig. 37).

31

36

37

29

38

39

Additional exercises

Once you are thoroughly warmed up, try these additional exercises.

Press-ups work the shoulders, the elbows, the upper arms and the muscles of the upper body. The basic press-up is performed with a straight back (fig. 38), and you may support your body weight on the flats of your hands, or on your knuckles. Growing children should not make a habit of pressing-up on their knuckles.

On the command, lower yourself down by flexing your elbows. Keep your body in a straight line and continue down until your chin grazes the floor (fig. 39). Pause briefly at that point before returning to the starting position.

The training effect of press-ups can be varied by changing the position of your hands. Move your hands in towards the centre-line and turn them so the fingertips face each other (fig. 40). Alternatively move your hands towards your waist and rotate them outwards.

There are still other ways in which you can perform press-ups. Try some out for yourself!

When you have done a number of these basic press-ups, go for explosive movement. After pausing at the lowest point, drive yourself up as quickly and forcefully as you can. The object is to clear the ground (fig. 41). Although pretty hard to do, this exercise is helpful in strengthening the action of punching.

Strengthen your back muscles by laying on your front and fully extending your arms and legs. On the command, arch your back and try to lift both your upper chest and your knees from the floor (fig. 42). Hold this position for a few seconds before relaxing back.

Lie on your back and draw up your knees. Lace your hands at the back of your neck. On the command, lift your upper back clear of the floor (fig. 43). Hold this position for a few seconds and then relax back in a controlled way. Pause at the lowest position and then repeat the exercise.

Alternatively, extend your legs out straight and on the command, lift both back and legs from the ground in what is called a 'vee-sit'

43

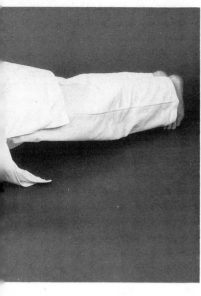

40

42

44

45

46

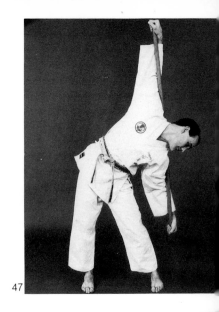
47

49

50

(fig. 44). Hold the flexed position for a few seconds before dropping back.

The spine is the supporting column of the body so it must be both flexible and strong. In the next two exercises, I have made use of a lightweight plastic pole or broom handle to fix the shoulders. Slide it behind your neck and drape your arms over it (fig. 45). Smoothly rotate your body (fig. 46) between its natural limits. Then lean your body from side to side (fig. 47).

Assisted stretches make use of a partner to apply controlled force. They should only be performed when you have properly warmed up.

The first stretch is based on an exercise I described earlier. Stand close to a support and raise your knee to the side. Remember the exercise? Your partner now takes your raised knee on top of his shoulder and braces it there (fig. 48). He applies firm upward pressure to open your legs still further while pulling down on the hip joint, but do not let him go past your own limit. When the point of actual discomfort is reached, tell him to stop. Notice that pressure is applied to the upper leg, so the knee is not stressed.

Try to relax the stretched muscles and that way, they can be persuaded to give a little more. When you have reached maximum stretch, extend your knee and point your toes (fig. 49). Keep your supporting foot flat on the floor and don't allow your heel to rise. Rotate your upper body away and prop yourself against the wall.

As an alternative, your partner stands behind you and supports your raised knee (fig. 50). He leans in against your lower back and draws your thigh backwards, so your leg wraps around his back and the quadriceps muscle on the front of the thigh is stretched. This is a good exercise to perform after running or kicking practice.

A partner can also assist box splits. Stand sideways-on to a support and straighten your leg, hooking your toes around the back of your partner's neck. If your hips aren't very supple, your partner should stoop, or even drop onto one knee to receive your foot. He then gradually stands up and you work at keeping your supporting foot flat on the floor (fig. 51). He steps back slightly, all the while giving you firm support. Take hold of the underside of your knee and pull your head forwards. Then turn your hips to the front, hooking your heel over his shoulder and pulling your head down (fig. 52).

This concludes the warm up section – you are now ready to begin training properly.

Beginning Training –
The Red Belt Syllabus

INTRODUCTION

I assume that you have read the previous chapters and gone through a proper warm-up. Now you are ready to begin karate training! Rather than snow you under with a lot of details too early on, I have divided this book into seven sections, each one corresponding to a kyu grade in the Ishin ryu training programme. It therefore follows that by the time you've reached the last section, you will have covered the programme to black belt.

Unfortunately, this book does not lend itself to analysing kata, so I have deferred that topic to another book.

STANCES

Open-toe stance
Begin training by learning a stance known as open-toe stance. The Japanese name for it is *musubi-dachi*, the word *dachi* being Japanese for 'stance'. Open-toe stance is a formal posture which you use when waiting to be told what you will be doing next. Stand with the heels of your feet together but the toes apart. Let your arms hang naturally close to your sides and extend the fingers (fig. 53).

Note the following points:

(a) Make sure your heels are touching.

(b) Hold your arms to your side.

(c) Keep your head up.

'Get ready' stance
Move from open-toe stance into 'get ready' stance. I call it by this name because it is the stance you take up in preparation for performing techniques. Its Japanese name is *fudo-dachi*. Step out to the left with your left foot, and to the right with your right foot. Your feet are shoulder-width apart, and turned slightly outwards. Let

54

55

your arms hang naturally by your sides as before, and clench your hands into fists (fig. 54).

Note the following points:

(a) Do not stand with your feet too wide apart.

(b) Take up a relaxed posture, since this is a stance from which fast movements can be unleashed.

Pigeon-toe stance

Pigeon-toe stance is a curious stance in which the feet are turned inwards. The Japanese call it *uchi hachiji-dachi* The feet are shoulder-width apart and the hips raised and brought forwards (fig. 55). If you are not performing any hand-technique from this stance, then just clench your fists and hold your arms away from the sides of your body.

Note the following points:

(a) The heels of both feet are in line.

(b) The toes are not turned too far inwards.

Hour-glass stance

Next take up hour-glass stance by stepping forwards and outwards a half-pace with your right foot. If you have stepped the correct distance, the heel of your right foot will be in line with the toes of your left foot. Keep both feet swivelled, so the toes continue to turn in. Lift your hips up and forwards. Relax your shoulders. In the illustration (fig.56), both arms have been brought up into a blocking position though they might equally as well be pulled back to the hips. The Japanese call this stance *sanchin-dachi*

Hour-glass stance is the stance from which a large number of basic techniques are performed. It formed the most frequently used stance

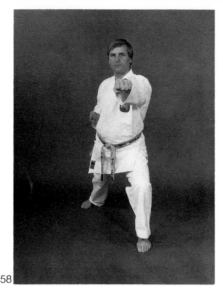

in the karate schools of Naha-te. When performed correctly, hour-glass stance is very strong and is able to resist pressure from all angles.

Move from one hour-glass stance to another by stepping inwards with the rear foot and then swinging it outwards. It takes a great deal of practice to maintain form whilst stepping from one hour-glass stance into another.

Note the following points:

(a) The heel of the leading foot is in line with the toes of the rear foot.

(b) Both feet are turned inwards.

(c) The hips are raised up.

Forward stance

Forward stance (its Japanese name is *zen kutsu-dachi*) is a powerful stance used during large movements. Step from 'get-ready' stance by withdrawing your right leg a full pace and a half. Your right knee extends but the sole of the foot otherwise remains pressed firmly to the floor. Your front knee is well bent, so it comes to lie above the toes. Because this is a fairly long stance, your hips will be turned three-quarters to the front and your left shoulder will lead slightly. A left punch has been adopted in the illustration (fig. 57), though when taking up the stance as part of basic training, it is more usual to use a lower parry guard. For just practising the stance, the fists may equally well be carried at the hips. The stance is not only long, it also has the dimension of width, so the feet are not in line (fig. 58).

If the right foot has moved inwards as well as backwards, then the stance will be narrow (fig. 59) and unstable. Even a light push will send you off balance (fig. 60). On the other hand, if you have stepped out to the side with your right foot, your stance will now be too wide (fig. 61) and a slight push forward on the shoulder will unbalance you (fig. 62).

61

62

65

66

If you step too far backwards with your right leg, then there will be insufficient weight on the front foot (fig. 63) and your punch will lack penetration. Also your front leg can easily be swept (fig. 64).

Your rear foot must be rotated so the toes point diagonally forwards. A common fault of novices is to rotate the rear foot so it points at ninety degrees to the leading foot (fig. 65). This withdraws the right hip and makes the stance unstable. A small push to the back will unbalance you diagonally forwards (fig. 66).

The instructor may well decide to test your stance, to make sure you have set it up properly. For example, he may apply pressure to your right leg (fig. 67) to ensure that the knee has been fully extended. I need hardly tell you that this form of testing is extremely dangerous and should only be carried out by someone who knows what he is doing, to someone who understands what is being tested for.

68

69

The second test checks that the body is braced and can withstand recoil. You should be able to resist pressure such as that shown (fig. 68) without staggering forwards. Similarly, your front foot should have sufficient body-weight over it to resist the drawing effect of a hooked foot (fig. 69).

The height of forward stance varies between styles of karate. Some styles use a high stance, whilst in others the stance is lower. I prefer a lower stance for a number of reasons, one of which is that it strengthens the muscles which hold the knee joint together. This is very important, considering the amount of work which the knee has to do during training.

Note the following points:

(a) The back knee is locked straight, the front knee is well bent.

(b) The front foot faces to the front and the rear foot is turned forwards as far as possible without the knee bending.

(c) The stance is both long and wide, so it is stable in all directions.

Whilst practising forward stance, it is as well to learn how to turn to face the reverse direction. Begin from forward stance (fig. 70) by swinging your rear foot across. Assume your leading foot is in the mid-line of this movement, and step an equal distance to the other side of this line. If you step too little, your new stance will be too narrow. If you step too far, your stance will be too wide.

Note that the rear knee is slightly flexed and only the ball of the foot is in contact with the floor (fig. 71). This gives a certain amount of spring to the turn. When your foot is correctly positioned, swivel your hips around and allow the shoulders to follow naturally. If you have stepped by the correct amount, your new stance will be set up correctly and require no adjustment (fig. 72).

71

72

Fighting Stance

The last stance to consider at this level is fighting stance (fig. 73). The Japanese name for this is *jiu-dachi*, or as it is sometimes known, *hanmei gamae*. This is useful stance from which a variety of attacks can be launched. It is not as long as forward stance, and there is less weight on the front foot. This makes it less stable but it allows for more rapid movement.

The front foot is rotated slightly inwards, so it is more or less parallel with the rear foot. This closes off the groin from direct attack. As you can see from the illustration, the body is not fully forwards-facing. The rear hip and shoulder are slightly withdrawn, reducing the size of target visible to an opponent (fig. 74).

Notice the way the hands are carried. The forward hand is held well forwards, in a position where it can stop attacks whilst they are still a distance from the target. The elbow is flexed so the leading fist is on a level with the shoulder and the arm is brought into the centre-line of the body.

The rear fist is held at chest height, where it can be used quickly to mount a counter attack. Don't pull the rear hand too far back, or it will be difficult to use it quickly when the need arises.

Turning from fighting stance is done in the same way as from forwards stance.

That concludes this first section on stances. Practise moving quickly from one stance into another, until you can take up any of them in left or right form, without hesitation. Use a mirror to check that your stance is set up correctly.

Punches and Strikes

Making a fist

Begin this section by learning how to make an effective fist. Fully open out your fingers and thumb (fig. 75). Bring the tips of the

75 76 77

79 80 81

fingers down until they touch the fleshy bar which runs along the base of the fingers (fig. 76). Roll the fingers into the palm (fig. 77) and lock index and middle fingers with the thumb (fig. 78).

If the fist has been correctly formed, then there will be a right angle between the upper joints of the folded fingers and the back of the hand (fig. 79). This is often difficult to achieve at first, but it will come after regular practice. Punching with a poorly formed fist (fig. 80) will soon skin the middle knuckles, so get the right shape by performing press-ups on the knuckles, or by punching against a bag, or against an impact pad made from hard foam plastic.

Notice the front view of the fist (fig. 81). The knuckles of the index and middle finger lead the others. This is because the fist is rounded and not flat, so not all the knuckles can make contact at the same instant. We use the first two knuckles in karate practice.

The fist is not held tightly all the time because this would be tiring

83

on the muscles of the lower arm. It would also slow down the speed of punching.

The fist must be held properly in relation to the wrist, so there is a straight line from the elbow to the tops of the knuckles (see fig. 79 once more). If the fist is twisted to one side (fig.82), or if it droops (fig. 83), then impact with a hard surface will cause it to flex painfully.

Practising a basic punch

Stand in hour-glass stance and extend your left arm. Form a fist and turn it so the palm faces towards the floor. Pull your right hand back to the hip, form a fist and rotate it so the knuckles face downwards (fig. 84). On the command, pull back your left fist whilst advancing the right one.

I always advise students to imagine that their fists are attached to each end of a piece of rope which passes from one fist, around a pulley, before coming back to the second. If you move one hand, the other must move at the same speed and over the same distance. It is the same with punching.

If your 'pulley' is working correctly, the fists will pass each other at the half-way point (fig. 85). As both fists reach the end of their movement, suddenly rotate your forearms, so the knuckles of the right fist turn upwards-facing and the knuckles of the left turn downwards (fig. 86).

This turning of the fists is an important factor in generating power. If you turn them too early, the elbows will move out from the body and straight line acceleration will be lost.

Another important factor is the speed with which you clench your fists. This must happen very quickly. Always punch into the centre-line of the body and aim at a constant height equivalent to the base of your breast-bone. If you could see yourself from above, you would see that your extended fist is at the crossing point of two imaginary lines extending from your feet.

The technique you have been practising is called a 'mid-section

85

86

87   88

punch', or *chudan-tsuki*. *Tsuki* is the Japanese word for punch, though in some applications it is spelt as *zuki*.

Powerful people often drive their shoulders in behind the punches. This is not necessary and leads to an unstable stance. A small shrug of the shoulders and a slight movement of the hip behind the punch are allowed. Punch with both hands, setting up a steady rhythm of practice. Do not slam your fists out hard because this may injure the elbow joints. Breathe rhythmically, expelling air sharply as you rotate and clench your fists.

In my clubs, this breathing out is turned into a loud shout, or *kiai*. When it is properly done, a kiai shows enthusiasm and strong motivation.

Repeat the punching sequence, but this time aim a little higher, as though you were punching to the face (fig. 87). This is a face punch, known as *jodan-tsuki* in Japanese. Then punch downwards towards the groin area. This is called *gedan-tsuki* (fig. 88).

Note the following points:

(a) The arms must always move together.

(b) Keep the elbows to your sides.

(c) Twist and clench your fists at the last instant.

(d) Use only slight shoulder and hip movement.

Punching to the jaw

The Japanese name for this technique is *seiken ago-uchi* (*uchi* meaning 'strike'). Any punch which connects forcefully to the side of the jaw (fig. 89) rotates the head sharply (fig. 90) and causes a knockout.

Begin practice from hour-glass stance and bring both fists up, so they are level with the tops of the shoulders. Hold them slightly away from the body (fig. 91). Lead in slightly with the right shoulder

as you simultaneously pull back the left. This brings the weight of your shoulder behind the punching arm (fig. 92). Having said that, don't lean in too much.

Do not twist your fist until contact is made, and then turn it strongly. Clench your fist tight on impact (fig. 93).

Back-fist
The basic punch is only one of several ways to use the clenched fist. You can also use the back of the knuckles in a technique which the Japanese call *uraken*. This technique is quite versatile, and can be used for both long, and short distance strikes. It generates power in quite a different way to the straight-line punches we have practised earlier. Back-fist travels in a circular manner, and this gives it a little more distance over which to accelerate. Delivery speed must be quite high and the fist is virtually thrown at the target.

94 95 96

(a) Back-fist to face   The Japanese name for this technique is *uraken ganmen-uchi*. It can be used from quite short distances and is effective against the bridge of the nose. Take up hour-glass stance and raise both fists in front of your face (fig. 94). Keep your elbows together. Use a slight amount of shoulder shrug to drive your right fist away from you. The elbow acts as a hinge for the strike, changing it from a straight-line punch, to a circular strike (fig. 95).

The fist is tightened sharply as it makes contact, and because the wrist is relaxed, the fist is snapped forwards into the target (fig. 96).

(b) Side back-fist to face   The Japanese name for this technique is *Yoko ganmen uraken uchi*. It works well when the attack comes from the side and you have no time to take up a new stance. In such cases, you must generate a lot of power regardless of how you find yourself. Stand in hour-glass stance and bring both fists together in front of your chest (fig. 97). Turn your head to get a clear view of the attacker and begin raising your right fist (fig. 98).

Your arm travels through an arc and the wrist is relaxed until you are about to make contact. Then bring your arm to a stop and let the wrist tilt forward (fig.99). Use this to attack the bridge of the opponent's nose (fig. 100).

(c) Side back-fist to the groin   The Japanese name for this is *uraken hizo-uchi* and as with the previous example, it can be used even when you aren't directly facing the attacker. This time hold your fists with the right resting on top of the left (fig. 101). Sharply turn your upper body into the target and let your right arm move back in an arc (fig. 102). Tighten your fist on impact (fig. 103). Use this strike to attack the opponent's groin (fig. 104).

Note the following points:

(a) Contact is made by a snapping action of the wrist.

101

97

98

9

100

02

103

104

(b) Contact is made with the back of the index and middle-finger knuckles.

(c) The strike travels in a partly circular manner to gain speed over a short straight-line distance.

Knife-hand

Knife hand uses the edge of the palm. It is effective because it concentrates a great deal of force over a small area. To avoid injury, strike with the part of your hand which lies between the base of your little finger and the top of the wrist. Stiffen your fingers as you are about to strike the target, and this will prevent them from jarring painfully against one another. It is permissible to bend the fingers slightly.

Knife-hand is quite versatile, and in this section we will see how it can be used to attack the side of the opponent's neck. The Japanese name for this is *shuto yoko ganmen-uchi*, where the word *shuto* means 'knife'.

105

Extend your left hand with the palm facing upwards. Slightly cup your fingers and tuck your thumb in. Your right hand is also opened into a knife hand, and it too has the palm facing upwards (fig. 105).

Bend your left elbow so your forearm lies along the front of your chest. Turn your left hand so the palm faces downwards. At the same time, draw back your right hand and bend the elbow, so your fingertips brush the back of your head (figs. 106 and 107). Notice how your upper body has rotated so the right shoulder is pulled back.

Pull your left arm strongly back across your chest and as you do so, let your shoulders swing round, so the striking hand travels in a wide circular path (fig. 108). Your shoulders continue to swing round until the left hand has been pulled back to your left hip, and your right hand has moved across the front of your body (fig. 109).

Although shoulder action plays only a small role in straight-line punches, it plays a much bigger part in circular strikes. For example, if you only swing your arm into this strike, you will not be able to project force into the impact and recoil will force your arm back (fig. 110).

Compare this with the second illustration (fig. 111), where the shoulder has rotated into the strike and the whole upper body is braced against impact.

Note the following:

(a) Stiffen the fingers on contact.

(b) Fold your thumb into the edge of your palm.

Lunge punch

To complete the section on strikes, we return to punches, but this time we practise them whilst moving up and down the dojo. The first of these punches is 'lunge punch', or *oi tsuki* as it is known in Japanese. It is effective because it adds the weight of the moving body to the power of the punch itself.

106

107

108

109

110

111

112

113

114

Begin practice from left forward stance (fig. 112) with your left arm extended. Both hands are closed into fists. Drive off the rear foot, so it slides forwards (fig. 113 and 114) and accelerates past the front foot. As a natural consequence of your step, your front foot will turn outwards slightly. Keep your shoulders motionless as you step and do not allow your arms to flap about. Maintain the same height throughout.

As you begin to put weight onto your front foot, pull back your left arm and punch with the right. Move your right hip behind the punch. Time everything so that your fists rotate and clench tight just as forward movement comes to a dead stop (fig. 115). Punch too early and you will throw yourself off-balance. Punch too late and you will lose all the energy of your moving body.

Repeat this sequence of punches, lunging forward on each leg alternately.

116

Note the following points:

(a) Don't bob up and down as you step.

(b) Don't swing your punching arm as you step.

(c) Throw your weight behind the punch.

Reverse punch
This is a form of lunge punch in which the opposite arm and leg lead. Its Japanese name is *gyaku-tsuki*.

Begin as for a lunge punch, in left forward stance, with left fist held out just above the left knee. I will explain the purpose of this guard in the section dealing with blocks. On the command, (*sono bade ippon-toru!*), punch without stepping forwards withdrawing your left fist to your left hip (fig. 116).

Step forwards with your right leg, so it slips past the left (fig. 117). Keep your height constant throughout the step and don't let your

120

48

shoulders move about. As you approach the final position, your right hip is lagging slightly back. Drive it forwards as you complete the punch, so your body faces completely to the front (figs. 118 and 119).

If your stance is too high when the punch is delivered (fig. 120), then recoil will lift your front foot and drive you backwards (fig. 121). Compare this with a longer stance in which weight is projected forwards. In this case, recoil is strongly resisted (fig. 122).

Many novices hunch their shoulders as they punch. This, too, is a bad fault because it ruins forward projection of weight and if pressure is applied to the punch, the whole upper body moves back (fig. 123). With the shoulder properly lowered and the arm in one straight line, no amount of reasonable pressure will buckle the arm (fig. 124). This is important when you are trying to deliver the full energy of your punch into the target.

123

124

125

126

Note the following points:

(a) Punch to the centre-line of your own body.

(b) Drive your hip behind the punch.

(c) Relax your shoulders.

BLOCKS

The third part of the programme concerns blocks. As already mentioned, these use a limb positioned so as to divert the attacking punch, strike or kick. In this section, we will practise three basic blocks.

127

Head block

There are two ways to block an attack to the head or face. One way is to deflect the attack upwards, the other way is to knock it to the side so it misses the target. In the first head block, we are going to deflect the attack upwards.

For our purposes, the Japanese word *uke* means 'block'. Therefore *jodan-uke* is a block which protects the head and face.

Begin from left forward stance and cross your forearms in front of your upper body (figs. 125 and 126). Hold your arms well out from the body. Continue the smooth upwards rise of your left arm, whilst pulling the right hand back to your hip (figs. 127 and 128). Remember the 'pulley principle'? Move your arms at exactly the same speed and clench both fists simultaneously.

Notice that the right fist also rotates, so the bony edge of the arm is

129

130

133

134

presented. Do not over-twist your forearm, or the sinews and veins of the wrist will be exposed to injury.

Notice the way your blocking arm is slightly flexed at the elbow. This allows a descending strike to glance harmlessly off. If you don't raise your blocking arm high enough, the attacker's fist may not be deflected sufficiently and hit you on the forehead (fig. 129). You may also close off your line of sight (fig. 130), so you are late in spotting a follow-up technique.

It is also possible to raise your blocking arm too high (fig. 131). This does not fully 'sweep' your head clear of attacking techniques.

A common fault often found when practising head block is that novices do not cross their forearms in front of their upper bodies. Withdrawing the non-blocking arm quickly not only makes the block more powerful, it also deflects attacks in its own right. Practise this by blocking the opponent's face punch with your left arm (fig. 132).

He then throws a fast left punch, which you stop with the arm you are withdrawing (fig. 133). The following block first catches (fig. 134) then sweeps the punch upwards (fig. 135).

Note the following points:

(a) Do not obscure your own vision.

(b) Twist your blocking arm on completion.

(c) Strongly pull back the non-blocking arm.

The second type of head block uses the inside part of the forearm to scoop the attacker's technique to the side. It is called 'inside head block', or *jodan uchi-uke*.

Begin from left forward stance and cross your arms over your

136

137

138

141

upper body (figs. 136 and 137). Note that both arms are rotated so the thumb-sides are touching the body. This is because both forearms must rotate as the block is applied.

Pull the right arm back strongly to a position on the hip. At exactly the same time, sweep the left arm up and out so it comes to rest with the fist at the same level as the top of your head, but slightly to the outside of it (figs. 138 and 139). The pull-through of the arms, moving as they do in opposite directions, lends a lot of power to the block. The rotation of both fists at the final instant gives the block a sharp impact, rather than a flaccid push.

You must sweep the attacking technique completely off to the side, otherwise it may still reach you (fig. 140). Keep your blocking elbow bent, so the forearm covers a lot of space as it moves.

As in the case of the basic head block, the arms cross-over acts as a safety precaution, so a fast punch is slowed right down (fig. 141) before it can be swept to the side (fig. 142).

Note the following points:

(a) Twist your forearm on blocking.

(b) Block right across your body.

(c) Strongly pull back the non-blocking arm.

Lower parry
This is a sweeping block covering the lower stomach and groin. It also uses the forearm, swinging it down in an arc, so the little finger side of the closed fist sweeps an attacking technique to the side. Its Japanese name is *juji gedan-barai*.

Begin from left forward stance, raising both forearms to the right side of your head, the right overlying the left (figs. 143 and 144). Clench your fists tightly. Throw your left arm diagonally downwards, so it sweeps across the lower body. As it reaches its final position, the right arm is drawn back strongly to the hip and the left

139

140

142

143

144

fist rotates so the little finger side of the hand is facing outwards (figs. 145 and 146).

The block finishes about two fist widths above the leading knee (fig. 147), and slightly to the outside of it (fig. 148).

The block must sweep right across the lower body, otherwise the attacking technique will be able to reach you (fig. 149). Keep your blocking elbow slightly bent to cushion the impact. The object is to meet the attack at an angle so it is swept to one side. Do not meet the attack full-on with your forearm, or you may break it!

Your fist must be fully rotated the correct way, otherwise it can flex painfully on impact.

Note the following points:

(a) Block away from the body.

(b) Sweep right across the front of your body – but don't over-block.

(c) Rotate your fist as you block, clenching it tight and folding the thumb in. Pull the non-blocking arm back to the hip.

KICKS

All parts of the foot are used as weapons. At this point in the programme, we will look at ways of using the instep and ball of the foot.

The instep

The instep is known as *haisoku* in Japanese. It is that area of the foot which lies between the base of the toes and the front of the ankle. To use it, you must extend your toes fully, turning them down slightly, so they are out of the way. Get the correct range and angle when you kick, otherwise you may strike with the toes, forcing them to bend painfully. Your ankle joint needs to be flexible, so it can extend fully. If you find if difficult to bring your shin and instep into one straight line, then you might try kneeling over periods of time, perhaps when watching television.

Most karate kicks are powered through the knee joint, so if you want strong techniques you must work at strengthening the muscles of the upper leg. Squats and leg-raises are good for this. You will also need hip flexibility so you can raise your knee both forwards and to the side.

(a) Kick to the groin   The word *geri* (or *keri*), is Japanese for 'kick'. *kin-geri* is the name for a kick to the groin (fig. 150).

Start from left forward stance and carry your hands in a relaxed but effective guard. Quickly bring your right knee up and forwards, at the same time swivelling on your supporting leg. Let your guard change as you do so (figs. 151a and 151b). Your knee rises at increasing speed until it is just above the level of your opponent's groin. Pull your toes down in preparation for impact.

151a

151b

152   153

Just as your knee reaches the correct height, kick out with your lower leg, so the foot makes an upward swing into the opponent's groin (figs. 152 and 153). Lean back slightly to keep your balance, or you will fall forwards into the opponent. Keep your shoulders low and do not wave your arms about.

Note the following points:

(a) The kick uses a fast, snapping action of the lower leg.

(b) The toes are pulled down so they won't be hurt on impact. The shin is in line with the instep.

Ball of foot
The Japanese term for the ball of the foot is *chusoku*. This refers to the pad of flesh immediately below the toes. To use this part of the foot it is necessary to pull back your toes. I leave my toes relaxed, so they can flex back by themselves on impact. Making a strong effort to pull your toes back will actually slow the kick.

(a) Front kick   Front kick uses the ball of the foot in a thrusting action. The shin must be in line with the instep, as it was with the groin kick but instead of the toes being turned down, they must be slightly lifted and relaxed (fig. 154). If you don't extend your foot enough (fig. 155), the ankle joint will absorb a lot of the impact.

Begin from left forward stance and raise your right foot quickly, bringing the knee upwards and forwards. To help this action, allow your supporting foot to swivel (figs. 156 and 157). When your knee reaches its correct height, thrust out the lower leg (figs. 158 and 159). The movement of the lower leg must merge with the action of the rising knee, otherwise the kick becomes jerky and a lot of power is wasted. Withdraw your kick before setting the foot down once more.

Carry your heel slightly low, so your relaxed toes flex back easily on impact (fig. 160). The object is to drive your foot into the target. If you find your foot skidding up the front of the target, then you have

155

156

159

161

not used your hips correctly. Project your hips forward and lean back slightly to keep your head above the supporting leg.

A good way to help you bring your knee high enough is to use a chair. Set this in front of you so you have to raise your knee high in order to let your foot pass over the chair (figs. 161 and 162).

Use front kick carefully or you will be counter-attacked. To see what I mean, try out the following sequence.

Stand facing your partner, both of you in left fighting stance (fig. 163). Bring your right knee up in preparation to use front kick. Your partner slides forwards on his front leg and reverse punches (fig. 164). As you can see, he is well within range.

Compare this with what happens if you withdraw your left foot slightly before raising your right knee (fig. 165). As your knee raises, your body is no longer brought so close to the opponent (fig. 166) and the punch falls short (fig. 167).

163

165

166

167

Note the following points:

(a) Bring the knee to the correct height.

(b) Bring your kicking leg close by the supporting leg – do not open your groin.

(c) Relax your shoulders and keep your arms still.

One-step front kick

This is used to close distance with an attacker. It is known as *tsurikomi-maegeri* in Japanese. Begin from left fighting stance, by taking a step forwards with the rear foot. Turn your right foot so the toes turn outwards-facing. Keep both knees bent so your height remains the same throughout (figs. 168 and 169). The length of your step must be adjusted to suit the distance you want to close.

Without pausing, as weight comes down onto the right foot, raise your left knee smoothly to kicking height and deliver a front kick (figs. 170 and 171). Withdraw the kick promptly after it has reached its target, and set the foot down carefully. If you do not keep your weight over your supporting leg, the momentum of your kicking leg will pull you forwards and off balance.

Novices often find that they hunch their shoulders during the step. This must be avoided. Maintain a relaxed but effective guard but don't let your arms flap about as you step.

Note the following points:

(a) Keep your height the same throughout the technique.

(b) Keep your arms to your side as you step.

(c) Set your foot down carefully after the kick.

171

172 173 174 175

High kick
Ke-age is the Japanese name for a high front kick. Practise it from left forward stance. Grip your fists firmly and hold your arms slightly out from your sides. Bring your right foot up and forwards, bending the knee slightly as you do so (fig. 172). Your foot continues its upwards swing until the knee touches the right shoulder (figs. 173 and 174).

The arms are held relaxed at the sides and they must not flap about during the kick. Keep your body upright and don't lean back, or the kick will lose height.

Knee kick to face
Knee kick to face (*hiza ganmen-geri*) is a very effective short-range weapon. Practise it from fighting stance by raising your rear knee up and forwards into the face. Hold your partner's head firmly in a double-handed grasp (fig. 175). Point your toes.

Alternatively, if you find yourself close-by and to the side of your opponent, grasp his sleeve and swing your knee both round and up into his solar plexus (fig. 176).

COMBINATIONS

As I have already explained, there isn't enough space in this book to cover the katas, so I am proceeding directly on to combinations.

Front kick, reverse punch.
This is the first of several combinations which you must learn. It is made up from two techniques, a front kick and a reverse punch. Both techniques are delivered to mid-section. The Japanese name for this is therefore *maegeri-chudan, gyaku-tsuki chudan*.

Begin from left fighting stance, launching a mid-section front kick. Make sure you kick to the centre and keep your shoulders relaxed throughout (fig. 177). Change your guard as you kick.

Withdraw the kick afterwards and set your foot down gently in a forward position (fig. 178). As the ball of your foot settles, use the energy of your still moving body to add power to the reverse punch (fig. 179).

Keep your elbows close to your side and don't twist your fist until your punch connects. Once your arm reaches full extension, withdraw it sharply and return it to the left hip. The other arm moves forwards to provide a front guard.

Note the following points:

(a) Punch and kick to the centre.

(b) Set the kick down carefully, don't just fall forwards on to it.

(c) Keep your face back as you punch.

178

179

180   181   182

One step front kick, reverse punch

The Japanese name for this is *tsurikomi-maegeri chudan, gyaku-tsuki chudan*. Begin from left fighting stance and step through in preparation for the kick (fig. 180). Notice how an effective guard is maintained throughout the movement. Deliver front kick to midsection with the rear leg (fig. 181) and perform a reverse punch on landing (fig. 182). Notice how the punch is delivered to the centreline of the opponent's body.

Note the following points:

(a) Keep a good guard throughout the combination.

(b) Maintain constant body height throughout the combination.

(c) Set your foot down carefully after the kick.

This concludes the techniques needed for the first part of the programme and we pass now to the second part.

The Yellow Belt Syllabus

With the exception of kata, we covered all the techniques needed for the first grading in the previous chapter. In this chapter we will go on to examine the techniques needed for the next grade. In Ishin ryu karate, that grade is identified by the yellow belt.

STANCES

Normal stance

Yellow belt grade introduces two new stances, the first of which is normal stance (*haisoku-dachi* in Japanese). This is a formal stance used at the beginning of certain forms of practice. Stand with your feet together for all of their length. Your arms hang down at your sides and your hands are clenched into fists (fig. 183). Hold your head up.

Note the following points:

(a) Your feet must be together for *all* of their length.

(b) Relax your shoulders.

Cat stance

This is a poised stance in which seventy per cent of the weight is concentrated over the back leg. The front leg rests lightly against the floor.

Slide your front foot forward by about a pace but don't allow it to move outwards. The leading foot points straight ahead, the rear foot is turned forty-five degrees outwards. Keep your body weight over the rear leg and bend the knee. Allow your front knee to bend slightly and raise your heel from the floor (figs. 184 and 185).

Note the following points:

(a) Keep your back straight and don't allow your bottom to stick out. Position your back directly above the heel of your rear foot. If you

184

185

186

187

188

do this correctly then most of your body weight will lie immediately above the supporting leg.

(b) Raise your front heel from the floor.

PUNCHES AND STRIKES

Roundhouse strike
Mawashi-uchi is the Japanese name for roundhouse strike. It is a powerful technique with good close-range applications. As you may know, the force of impact is related to the speed at which your strike is travelling and over a short distance there is sometimes not enough space to accelerate fully in a straight line.

Roundhouse strike gets over this in a novel manner – by taking the strike out and around in a circle.

Despite the added distance over which the strike must travel, its curving path makes it difficult to block. If the opponent attempts to evade and moves the wrong way, then he will actually move into it. Even if he moves the correct way, the strike can literally curl around a blocking arm and still strike the target.

Stand in hour-glass stance and bring your left arm up so the elbow is flexed and the fist lies just above the forehead. Rotate the fist so the thumb-side is facing downwards. Pull your right hand back to your hip (fig. 186). On the command, drop your left elbow and pull it back to your right hip (fig. 187).

Use your left arm to add power to the strike, pulling it back strongly as you allow the right to rise away from the hip (fig. 188), rotating to thumb-downwards position as it does so. Notice the wide, curving path that the fist is following.

Because your arms are moving together, the left fist comes to a stop on the left hip as the right fist comes to a stop (fig. 189). Clench both fists tightly as the technique is completed.

Use this technique to attack the side of the opponent's head (fig. 190).

189

190

191

192

196

Note the following points:

(a) Move both arms together.

(b) Clench both fists tightly on impact.

Knife-strike

(a) Knife-strike to the collarbone   *Shuto sakotsu-uchi* is the Japanese name for a descending knife hand strike to the opponent's collarbone (fig. 191). This too uses a circular motion. The strike can also be applied to the opponent's bicep.

Begin from hour-glass stance and extend your left arm, turning the fingers upwards and presenting the edge of the hand (fig. 192). Your right hand is held against the right side of your body, with the palm turned upwards and the fingers extended.

Fold your left arm across the front of your chest and bring your right arm up and behind your head (fig. 193). Notice how the fingers of the right hand are turned downwards.

Power for the strike comes from the pulling back of the left arm to its final position on the left ribs. As it is being pulled back, the right arm curves past the side of your head and descends towards the target (fig. 194). As your left hand comes to a stop, your right does too (fig. 195).

(b) Knife-strike to the spleen   *Shuto hizo-uchi* is an effective strike to the lower ribs on the left side of the body (fig. 196). It travels in the now familiar curved path – this time in such a way as to drive between the opened ribs. Striking in the right spot and with enough power will damage the spleen and can result in injury! So please exercise care when practising this technique with a partner.

Begin as before from hour-glass stance and extend your left hand forwards and downwards, the palm facing upwards (fig. 197). Your right hand is held against the ribs, with the palm facing upwards.

Rotate your left palm so it turns downwards, and pull it across your chest, so the elbow faces forwards. Bring your right hand up and behind your head (fig. 198).

Withdraw your left arm and let your shoulders swing round with the developing strike (fig. 199). As your left hand pulls to a stop, your right is tightened into knife-hand (fig. 200).

(c) Thrusting knife-hand strike to the solar plexus Not all knife-hand strikes follow a circular path. Some like *shuto uchi-komi* travel in a straight-line, similar to that used with some punches. This particular technique is an effective thrust to the opponent's solar plexus (fig. 201).

Take up hour-glass stance and extend your right arm. Turn your right wrist so the fingers point upwards and the thumb is closed across the palm. The edge of the palm faces the opponent. Carry the

201

202

203

204

left hand palm-upwards facing against your ribs (fig. 202).

On the command, drive out your left hand, rotating it through ninety degrees, so the thumb is upwards-facing. Make use of the pulley principle to pull back the right hand at the same time (fig. 203). Thrust your left hand into the strike whilst withdrawing the right to your side. Tense your muscles sharply to give a little extra thrust at the end of the strike (fig. 204).

Punching and kicking on the move

(a) Mid-section kick, mid-section punch   We now continue training in how to kick and punch whilst moving forwards. The first sequence to practise is mid-section kick, mid-section punch (*kette chudan-tsuki* in Japanese). Take up left forward stance and extend your left arm, straightening the elbow (fig. 205). Drive off your right leg and quickly

raise your knee to kicking height for front kick. Do not hunch your shoulders and keep your extended punching arm quite still (figs. 206 and 207).

Withdraw your kick but maintain controlled forwards momentum. Place your foot carefully (fig. 208), and as weight descends on it drive out your right arm whilst withdrawing the left (fig. 209).

The following are common faults to avoid when performing this sequence:

(a) Lifting the shoulders as you kick.

(b) Waving your arms about.

(c) Not bringing your kick high enough. There should only be a small gap between your fist and the kicking leg.

206

207

208

209

210

211

212

213

(d) Landing too heavily after the kick. Keep control over your centre of gravity.

(e) Failing to punch at the correct time, i.e. when weight is settling down on the ball of the kicking foot.

If you are training alone, use a mirror to show up any faults.

(b) Mid-section kick, mid-section reverse punch   The Japanese name for this is *kette chudan gyaku-tsuki*. Begin from left forward stance and extend your left fist forwards in a basic punch. Punch without stepping, and in so doing, drive your punching hip forwards (fig. 210).

Keep your shoulders still as you perform a front kick to mid-section (fig. 211), then withdraw the kick and set it purposefully down in the right place. As weight descends on the ball of your right heel (fig. 212), twist your left hip in behind the reverse punch (fig. 213).

Faults to watch out for are the same as those listed for the previous technique. Additionally, avoid landing in too long a stance and not being able to project the hips into the punch.

BLOCKS

Mid-section outer block
Chudan soto-uke is a powerful circular block which knocks attacks to the side. It generates its force by accelerating along a circular path.

Begin from hour-glass stance, raising your left fist in front of your chin and flexing your elbow through ninety degrees. Lead slightly with your left shoulder and draw back your right fist (fig. 214). Drop your left forearm back along your chest and raise your right fist up and behind your head (figs. 215 and 216).

Pull back your left arm, so your shoulders swing round, carrying

215

216

217

218

219

the blocking arm with them (fig. 217). Notice that the palm is turned outwards until the last possible instant, when it sharply rotates into blocking position (fig. 218). Both arms stop moving together, the fists clenching tight to add extra force (fig. 219).

Follow the block with a strong reverse punch to mid-section. Withdraw your blocking arm to the hip to lend power to the punch.

Check for the following faults:

(a) The most common fault is not to bring your blocking arm far enough across the front of your body, so an attack is not fully deflected (fig. 220).

(b) Don't let your fist lead your elbow as it sweeps across the front of your body. Fist and elbow must be in one line, otherwise the attack may not be properly blocked.

(c) Don't block past the front of your body. This is unnecessary and pulls your blocking shoulder too far forwards, making it difficult to follow-up quickly with a reverse punch.

(d) Focus the block's force to one point, so it doesn't just fizzle out.

Double blocks

Inside upper block and lower parry (*jodan uchi-uke, gedan barai*) is a combination of two blocks performed simultaneously. The effect of this is to sweep a large area of attacking techniques. Used correctly, it protects the face and the entire upper body.

Start from hour-glass stance with your right arm raised and flexed ninety degrees at the elbow. Extend your left arm diagonally downwards and straighten your elbow (fig. 221). Note that both blocks are slightly wider apart than shoulder-width.

222   223   224

On the command, bring your right arm smartly down and across the front of your chest. As this happens, bring your left arm up, so the two cross-over at chest height (fig. 222). The left arm continues rising as the right travels on down into a lower parry. Both arms stop abruptly at the same time (fig.223).

Note the following points:

(a) Both arms must travel in complete semi-circles. Many beginners simply lift one arm straight up whilst lowering the other and there is no proper cross-over in the middle.

(b) As you repeat the block, take care that your blocking arms do not separate too widely. Shoulder-width is the distance to aim for.

(c) Hold the lower parry well out from the body – don't let it flop back against the stomach.

This combination block is useful against a double-handed grasp of your lapels (fig. 224). Bring your right arm diagonally across the opponent's arms, whilst your left arm bars across the underneath (fig. 225). Drive your right arm down between the opponent's arms, whilst bringing your left arm up and through (fig. 226). Provided you use a little power, he will be forced to release his grip, and you can perform a left reverse punch (fig. 227). If necessary, follow-up with a second reverse punch.

Knife blocks
Knife-hand makes a good block as well as being an effective strike. Many styles of karate use it to deflect an attacking technique. Its Japanese name is *shuto-uchi* and it can be employed at head height, mid-section or the lower stomach. The first two are the most frequently encountered and it is these we shall consider here.

(a) Knife block to head *Jodan shuto-uke* uses a vertical blocking forearm with the extended fingers pointing directly upwards (fig.

25   226   227

28   229

228). By comparison, *chudan shuto-uke* is often practised with the blocking forearm leaning forwards (fig. 229).

Jodan shuto-uke can be practised from cat stance. Assuming you begin from left stance, raise your left arm and bring your right hand palm-upwards facing across your chest (fig. 230). Step forwards a short distance with your right foot and lower your blocking arm so the palm faces downwards. At the same time, bring your right arm across your body, so the palm brushes your left ear (fig. 231). Complete the step and rotate your shoulders away from the block. Draw back your left hand and rotate it so the palm faces upwards. As this happens, your right arm moves forwards and rotates so the palm faces forward (fig.232).

Note the following points:

(a) Keep your fingers pointing vertically upwards. The blocking

230   231   232

forearm must be vertical in all planes – not just from front to back, but from side to side also.

(b) Move smoothly through the step and time the blocking action so it concludes exactly as you settle into the new stance.

(c) Rotate your body away from the blocking action. This fixes the shoulders and gives the block additional force.

(d) Rotate both forearms at the same time, so the block finishes sharply.

Mid-section knife block is delivered in exactly the same way. The pull-through motion is as before, except that the blocking forearm is now leaning forwards. This technique is most commonly practised from what is called 'back stance' (see page 110).

23

(b) Roundhouse knife-block   *Shuto mawashi-uke* is an effective circular block which covers a large area. Both arms move in a circular path and use the palm-edge as the blocking surface.

Begin from left cat stance and extend the left hand into a knife-block. Note that the hand is carried well forwards and the elbow is almost straight. The right hand is held against the chest with the palm facing upwards (fig. 233). On the command, both arms are extended and the hands rotated so the palms face downwards (fig. 234). Draw them back and upwards (fig. 235) in a wide circle that takes them past the side of the head (fig. 236 and 237).

The circle continues with the left arm extending out as it drops, the right falling back to a position on the chest (fig. 238). The movement finishes on both hands simultaneously. Note that both hands are moving together for much of the block.

Use this technique to draw out and deflect a punch (fig. 239), then to continue into a knife hand strike against the opponent's face (figs. 240 and 241).

234

235

236

237

238

239

240

243

The same action will also lift and draw out a kick (figs. 242 and 243). As the circular movement continues, the opponent loses balance and falls backwards (fig. 244).

Kicks

Stamping kick
Mae-kansetsu geri is a stamping kick, used to attack the knee joint. It is a particularly dangerous technique and great care should be taken when practising it with a partner.

Stamping kick strikes with the heel and the outer edge of the foot. The foot is pulled into a right angle with the shin and the big toe is raised whilst the others are turned downwards (fig. 245).

241

242

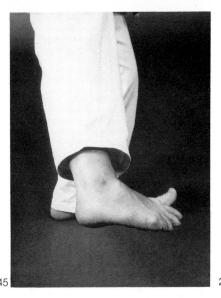

245

246

247

248

Stand sideways to your partner, and separate your feet by a shoulder-width or so. Bend your knee and draw up the leading leg. Point your heel at the opponent's kneecap (fig. 246) and drive your foot straight down. Lean away to keep your balance (fig. 247). Project your hip into the kick and allow your supporting foot to slide in the same direction (fig. 248). This adds extra force to the impact. Withdraw your foot afterwards and set it down carefully.

Note the following points:

(a) You must turn your foot so you strike with the heel and the outer edge of the foot. Do not strike with the flat of your foot.

(b) Don't allow your foot to flop around, or it will be injured. Anchor it firmly as it is about to make contact.

(c) Raise your knee high enough, so the kicking foot descends on the target. By this means the weight of the leg adds to the power of its muscles.

(d) Keep your arms to your sides as you kick. Many people flap their arms about.

(e) Lean back to keep your balance, otherwise you will fall forward into your opponent as you kick.

Front kick to the head

The Japanese name for this technique is *maegeri-jodan*. It is performed as for a normal front kick. Begin from forward stance and bring your rear knee up and through. Raise it high, otherwise your kick will be too low (fig. 249). Change your guard as the knee comes through. Lean back slightly to balance the weight of your kicking leg but never let your head go beyond an imaginary vertical line from the heel of your supporting leg (fig. 250). Drive the kick into the opponent's face (fig. 251).

Note the following points

(a) Pull your toes back.

(b) Don't open your groin as you kick. The kicking leg should brush past the supporting leg.

(c) Kick to the centre-line of an imaginary opponent's body.

(d) Keep your arms to your side as you kick, and don't hunch your shoulders.

(e) Maintain your balance throughout so you can set your foot down carefully after the kick.

251

252

Snap kick to jaw

Ago-maegeri is rather like a cross between *keage* and *maegeri-jodan*. The ball of the foot is used, but the kicking knee is raised very high and kept close to the chest. From there the lower leg is driven upwards and out, making contact with the underneath of the opponent's jaw (fig. 252).

Roundhouse kick to mid-section

Roundhouse kick is one of the most popular kicking techniques in karate. In this version, the instep (*haisoku*) is delivered to the opponent's mid-section (fig. 253). The Japanese term used to describe this techique is *mawashi-kubi* (or *haisoku*)-geri.

254

Begin from right forward stance, bringing your left leg up to the side (fig. 254 and 255). Point your toes and allow the supporting leg to swivel. Maintain smooth acceleration through the technique so that as the supporting leg swivels even more, the bent kicking knee is brought right across the front of your own body (figs 256 and 257). As the knee actually comes to point directly at the target, the lower leg is driven out (figs. 258 and 259). Withdraw the foot after impact and set it down.

Note the following points:

(a) The kicking foot must accelerate smoothly throughout the whole movement to the point of impact, with no hesitation or jerkiness.

(b) The kicking knee must rise smoothly to the correct height.

(c) The supporting foot must be allowed to swivel freely so that it actually comes to face the other way as the kick is delivered. This frees the hips and allows them to work properly.

(d) The upper body must lean away from the kick, so as to counterbalance the extending leg. The arms must not be allowed to wave about. The head is raised.

253

5

256

257

258

259

260   261

(e) The kicking foot must be held firm on impact, after which it must be set down carefully.

Without doubt, the major problem that novices have with round-house kick stems from lack of flexibility at the hip joint. Few new students can raise their knees to the required height and those who cannot must cheat. Either the hip is not turned far enough, and the kick turns into a variety of 'diagonal front kick' (fig. 260), or the hip turns too far and the knee faces towards the floor (fig. 261).

COMBINATIONS

One-step front kick, mid-section reverse punch
The Japanese expression for this combination is *tsurikomi maegeri, gyaku-tsuki chudan*.

Begin from fighting stance and take a step forwards with the rear leg (fig. 262). Adjust the length of your step to suit the distance you wish to cover. Bring your kicking knee up sharply and deliver a front kick to mid-section (fig. 263). Set the kicking foot down carefully and perform a reverse punch (fig. 264). Withdraw the punch smartly afterwards.

Note the following points:

(a) Don't hunch your shoulders as you step.

(b) Don't let your arms flap around.

(c) Accelerate smoothly through the step.

(d) Punch as you are landing and aim for the centre-line. Withdraw the punch and re-establish your guard.

Roundhouse kick to mid-section, reverse punch to mid-section
The Japanese name for this is *mawashigeri-chudan, gyaku-tsuki chudan*.

263

264

265

266

Bring your rear leg up and forwards to deliver mid-section roundhouse kick (fig. 265). Lean back to maintain balance but keep your head up and set your foot down carefully. As you settle weight onto your foot, drive out a reverse punch (fig. 266), and retrieve it afterwards.

Note the following points:

(a) The hips must turn fully during the kick – no short-cuts!

(b) The foot must be properly retrieved before it is set down.

(c) The hip twists fully in the opposite direction to deliver the reverse punch – don't rely just on shoulder action.

(d) Both kick and punch must be to the centre-line of the body.

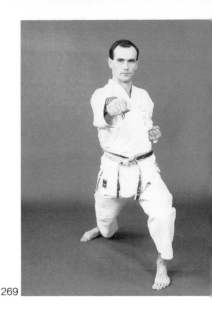

267   268   269

One-step roundhouse kick to mid-section, reverse punch to mid-section
The Japanese name for this is *tsurikomi-mawashigeri chudan, gyaku-tsuki chudan*.

Begin with a step forwards from fighting stance (fig. 267). Swivel your hips and perform a roundhouse kick to mid-section (fig. 268). Withdraw the kick and set it down deliberately, then follow with a reverse punch to mid-section (fig. 269). Withdraw the punch immediately afterwards.

This concludes the techniques needed for this part of the training programme.

The Orange Belt Syllabus

Straddle stance
There are two new stances to learn in this chapter. The first is a variety of straddle stance called *kiba-dachi*. To adopt straddle stance, step out to the left and right, so your feet are wider than shoulder-width by about half a step. Your feet are turned slightly inwards but the knees are rotated outwards. Your back must be straight and your bottom tucked in.

A low straddle stance is difficult to maintain at first, but it is useful for strengthening the muscles on the front of the thighs. These in turn, strengthen the knee joints and help protect them from injury during kicking practice. Some schools of karate use straddle stance as an alternative to hour-glass stance for basic punching practice.

These are the main points of the stance:

(a) The body's centre of gravity must be over the middle of the stance.

(b) The lower legs must rise vertically from ankles to knees; they must not slope inwards.

(c) Body weight is taken on the outside edges of the feet.

(d) The back must be upright.

One-legged stance
This is a curious stance, used briefly when delivering a side-kick or avoiding a foot-sweep. Its Japanese name is *tsuruashi-dachi*. Sometimes it is called 'crane on a rock stance', or simply 'crane stance'. The crane is represented in several martial arts systems.

Lift one knee high and to the side of your body, and balance on the supporting leg (fig. 270). If you then want to use side kick, pull your kicking foot into the correct shape.

270

271

272

273

274

Punches and Strikes

Lower thrust punch
This is a short-range punch to the body, known in Japanese as *shita-tsuki*. The fist does not rotate fully.

Stand in hour-glass stance and extend your right fist forwards. The fist lies in the centre-line of the body and is turned so that the palm faces upwards. The elbow is bent and held close to the body (fig. 271).

On the command, twist your right fist sharply palm-downwards (fig. 272) then withdraw it as you thrust the left fist out (fig. 273). Turn it palm-upwards again and clench both fists tightly as the punch connects (fig. 274).

Note the following points:

(a) The punching elbow must not fully straighten.

(b) Only the withdrawing fist rotates.

(c) The elbows stay close to the sides of the body.

Hammer-fist strike
The fist can be used in a variety of ways, such as hammer-fist strike, or *tettsui-uchi*. Though the fist is made in the usual manner, the area of contact is not the front of the two large knuckles; it is the pad of flesh between the little finger knuckle and the wrist. The strike gets its name from the way that the fist is used (figs. 275 and 276).

Take up hour-glass stance and extend your left fist, turning it so the thumb is uppermost. Your right hand is also clenched into a fist and is carried palm upwards-facing (fig. 277). Take your left arm back across your chest so the elbow points forward. Lift your right hand up and behind your head (fig. 278).

Draw back your left arm strongly to give added power to the strike.

5

6

277

278

93

279

280

281

282

283

284

Your right hand moves over the top of your head and strikes down into the target. Both fists clench tightly and come to a simultaneous stop (fig. 279).

Hammer-fist need not only be used in a downwards strike; it can also be used in a flat, circling strike to the side of the head (fig. 280).

Take up hour-glass stance and extend your left arm. Bend your elbow and rotate your fist so the knuckles face downwards (fig. 281). Pull your right arm back to your side. Take your left arm back across your chest and raise your right, taking it to the side of your jaw (fig. 282). Turn the knuckles towards you. Pull back your left arm and use shoulder action to swing the right arm around (fig. 283). Rotate your knuckles just before impact, so the palm turns upwards (fig. 284).

Note the following points:

(a) You must pull back the non-striking fist quickly.

285

94

(b) Allow your shoulders to swing freely with the strike.

(c) Rotate the striking fist just as it is about to make impact.

Palm-heel strike

Palm heel (*shotei*) is an effective weapon because the bones are cushioned by a pad of muscle, and the wrist joint is less likely to flex painfully on contact. It can be used in the same manner and at the same targets as a straight-line punch (fig 285), or it can be used as a short distance strike.

To make palm-heel, flex your fingers so the tips brush against the pad of flesh which runs across the top of the palm. Fold your thumb in so it won't get caught in someone's sleeve! Flex your wrist back as far as it will go (fig. 286).

Spear-hand

Though spear-hand looks at first glance like knife-hand, it is used in a completely different way. Knife-hand uses the edge of the palm in a chopping action; spear-hand uses the tips of the fingers in a jabbing motion. The hand is fully extended and the thumb folds across the palm. The middle finger is withdrawn, so as to spread the impact over three fingers (fig. 287). The hand tenses on impact.

The Japanese name for spear-hand is *nukite*.

There are a number of different forms of spear-hand, one of which uses two fingers to attack the eyes. The index and middle fingers are stiffened on impact whilst the others fold into the palm (fig. 288).

Spear-hand strike is made with a thrusting action that takes the tips of the fingers into the eyes (fig. 289). On impact, the fingers can curl so they lodge in the eye sockets. The thumb locks under the chin (fig. 290).

It goes without saying that great care should be used when practising this technique with a partner.

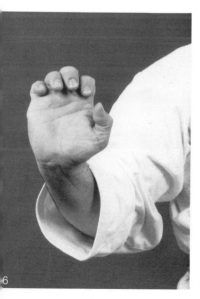
6

287

288

BLOCKS

Augmented forearm block

The Japanese name for this block is *morote-uke*. It uses both arms together, one strengthening – or 'augmenting' – the other. Begin practice from left forward stance and raise your left arm, flexing the elbow through ninety degrees. Bring your other arm up and push the right fist into your left elbow (figs. 291 and 292).

Move into right forward stance and as you do so, allow both arms to fall to your left side (fig. 293). Keep your arms close together. As you settle into the new stance, swing both arms up together, jamming your left fist into your right elbow (fig. 294).

Note the following points:

(a) The blocking forearm must be vertical and the supporting forearm must be horizontal.

292

293

294

295

296

297

298

(b) Drop both arms the instant you advance and swing them back up to a stop as your stance change completes. Avoid a 'one-pause-two action'.

(c) The block uses a lot of hip and shoulder action. Don't just rely on the forearms.

(d) Block right across the front of your face and bring both arms to a clean and abrupt stop.

Augmented forearm block can be used in a number of situations, the following being one example:

An opponent has seized your lapel with his left hand (fig. 295). Bring your right arm underneath his arm (fig. 296). Swing both arms up and knock his hand away with an augmented block (fig. 297). Your right fist is close to the opponent's face, so punch him (fig. 298).

299 300

Lower parry

We have already practised a form of lower parry (see page 55) but this is a slightly different form. The Japanese name for it is *mae-gedan barai*.

Begin from left forward stance or hour-glass stance and extend your right fist diagonally downwards, so it comes to rest above and slightly to the outside of your leading knee. Bring your left arm up, so the lower knuckles of the fist rest against your right shoulder (figs. 299 and 300).

Pull your right fist back to your right hip, using this action to help straighten the left elbow (figs. 301 and 302). As your arm straightens, turn your shoulders and hips slightly away. Then drive your hips and shoulders forwards as you reverse punch to mid-section (fig. 303).

Note the following points:

(a) The block is delivered from a flexed elbow. The fist rotates only as the arm is coming to a stop – not before.

(b) Both arms stop moving together, so there is a crisp finish to the block.

(c) Block so your arm comes to lie just above your knee. If your arm doesn't come far enough across, then an attack can still reach you (fig. 304).

(d) Do not over-block so your arm moves too much to the side. Don't block with your arm too close to your thigh, and don't block with your arm held too high. All of these errors will reduce the block's effectiveness.

In the illustration, your extended right arm locates the kick (fig. 305) and your left arm blocks it (fig. 306). Complete the sequence with reverse punch (fig. 307).

301

302

303

305

306

100

307

308

Note that the block does not meet the kick full-on; rather it strikes the side of the leg. This deflection is enough to turn the opponent, opening him to a reverse punch.

KICKS

Side kick to mid-section
The Japanese name for this technique is *yoko-geri chudan*. Like the stamping kick to the knee (page 84), this kick uses the heel and outer edge of the foot, but this time the target is the opponent's mid-section (fig. 308).

The technique requires good hip flexibility because the upper leg must be lifted so the heel is at the same height as the target. This allows a straight thrusting action, which makes the kick extremely

312

311

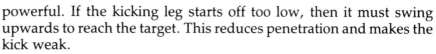

powerful. If the kicking leg starts off too low, then it must swing upwards to reach the target. This reduces penetration and makes the kick weak.

Go into left forward stance and bring your right knee up and forwards. Pull your big toe up and turn the other toes downwards. Bring your kicking knee diagonally across the front of your body, allowing the supporting leg to pivot at the same time (figs. 309 and 310). Throw your hips into the kick as you drive the heel out (figs. 311 and 312).

Note the following points:

(a) Your kicking heel must be at the correct height. If it is too low (fig. 313), then instead of travelling straight into the target it will curve upwards and perhaps miss it altogether.

103

(b) Thrust your hips into the kick for extra penetration.

(c) If you straighten your supporting leg, recoil will knock you back off balance (figs. 314 and 315).

Mid-section roundhouse kick using ball of foot
The Japanese name for this technique is *mawashigeri chudan chusoku*. It is similar to the kick we studied on page 86 except that here, impact is made with the ball of the foot (fig. 316).

Take up right forward stance and raise your knee diagonally to kicking height (fig. 317). Allow your supporting leg to turn freely. As your knee comes into line (fig. 318), drive the lower leg out and into the target (fig. 319). Withdraw the kick after impact by flexing the knee and set the foot down carefully.

314

315

316

317

318   319

Note the following points:

(a) The kicking leg accelerates smoothly from the floor, into the target. There must be no hesitation or jerkiness.

(b) The supporting leg must swivel freely, and the upper body must lean back to allow proper hip action to occur. Keep your head up.

(c) Impact is made with a thrusting action of the leg – not just a passive swinging action.

(d) The guard must be maintained throughout.

Sparring

The Japanese word for sparring is *kumite*. There are different kinds of sparring practice, the most simple being where the attacker and the defender use pre-arranged moves. This allows them to test their techniques in a controlled way.

It is one thing knowing how to kick a punchbag, and another to kick an opponent. A punchbag doesn't have elbows and knees to get in the way!

Simple pre-arranged sparring is a safe way to practise the blocks we have been studying. We know what the attack will be, and we know which block is to be tested, so we can see if it actually works. Even this level of controlled sparring can show up failures in technique.

It is best to begin sparring with someone of your own size. Decide who is going to attack first and when you are both ready, make the first attack. Stay as you are for a couple of tries because this will allow more efficient learning to take place, then change over.

There are as many sparring situations as there are techniques. The following are merely examples of how you can practise your blocks. In this case, we are using what are called 'scooping blocks'.

320

321

322

323

Outer scooping block

Outer scooping block (*soto harai-uke*) is performed from fighting stance (fig. 320). As you see the opponent's knee lifting, step outwards with your front foot (fig. 321) and make ready to block with your leading hand. The side-step takes your body out of the direct line of the kick.

Twist your hips so your body turns completely through ninety degrees. Bring your leading arm smartly across your body with fingers extended, and slap the kick to one side (fig. 322). Before the opponent has time to collect himself, twist your hips once more and deliver reverse punch (fig. 323).

Don't step too much to the side or you will be unable to follow up the opponent's attack with an immediate counter-attack of your own.

Note that the block depends on hip action. First the hips rotate one way, then the other. Without this movement, both block and punch are weak. You will only be able to learn this technique properly if the kick is actually aimed at you. Start off slowly, and only increase speed when your partner develops confidence.

Inner scooping block

This version is also practised from fighting stance. As your opponent's knee rises to deliver front kick, take a diagonal step back and outwards with your rear leg (fig. 324). This withdraws your body from the direction of the kick. Quickly draw up your trailing leg and deflect the kick (fig. 325).

Attack with an immediate reverse punch before your opponent has time to recover (fig. 326).

As with the previous block, you should not step too far to the side, otherwise there's no need to block at all. It will also take too long for you to close distance and counter-attack.

4

325

326

327

328

329

330

Withdraw your trailing leg, so that it doesn't get trodden on when the unsuccessful kick lands.

COMBINATIONS

Front kick, roundhouse kick, reverse punch
The Japanese name for this is *maegeri chudan, mawashigeri chudan, gyaku-tsuki chudan.*
Perform front kick from fighting stance (fig. 327), withdrawing it before you set it down. Rotate your hips and perform a roundhouse kick to mid-section (fig. 328). Since a particular form of roundhouse kick hasn't been asked for, use either the instep or ball-of-foot variety. As you set the kick down (fig. 329), make a reverse punch with your rear hand (fig. 330), withdrawing it afterwards.

Note the following points:

(a) Maintain a constant speed throughout the combination, avoiding hesitation and jerkiness.

(b) Don't blur one technique into the next. Each technique must be properly performed.

One-step front kick, roundhouse kick, reverse punch
The Japanese name for this combination is *tsurikomi-maegeri chudan, mawashigeri chudan, gyaku-tsuki chudan.* It is performed in the same manner as the previous combination, except for a step before the first kick.

108

The Green Belt Syllabus

STANCE

Open stance

The Japanese name for this open stance is *heiko-dachi*. The feet are less than shoulder-width apart, and are parallel for all of their length. The knees are straight and the body upright. The hands hang naturally to the sides (fig. 331).

Straddle stance

We previously described a form of straddle stance on page 91. This later stance is an alternative, and is much used by the giant sumo wrestlers of Japan. For this reason, it is sometimes called 'sumo stance'. Its Japanese name is *shiko-dachi*.

Step out to the side with both left and right feet, so the stance becomes about one and a half shoulder-widths wide. Allow your feet to turn out slightly, so they are in line with the thighs (fig. 332). There is no twisting action on the knee joints, and this will be appreciated by those karateka with damaged knees!

331

332

333   334

Note the following points:

(a) The back must be straight and the bottom tucked in (fig. 333).

(b) The knees are directly above the ankles.

(c) The feet are turned slightly outwards.

Back stance

We talked briefly about this stance when we discussed using knife block to mid-section (page 80). The front foot points forwards but the back leg is turned more than ninety degrees to the side. The heels of both feet are nearly in line and the centre of gravity is moved towards the back leg. Having said that, the weight bias is not as extreme as in cat stance.

The back leg supports sixty per cent of the weight, the front leg, forty per cent. Both feet are flat on the floor (fig. 334).

Note the following points:

(a) The back is upright, and there is no lean in any direction.

(b) The hips are turned threequarters to the side.

(c) Both knees are bent.

PUNCHES AND STRIKES

Vertical punch

If we examine the way a basic karate punch behaves, we will see that it goes through three stages. The first is as it leaves the hip and travels to the half-way position. At this stage, it has not begun to rotate, so the palm faces upwards (fig. 335). Remember how we described this as 'close punch' (*shita-tsuki*) on page 93.

335

As the punch approaches the target, it begins to rotate to a palm-down position. However, if we stop the rotation at the half-way point (figs. 336 and 337), we have a technique referred to as 'vertical fist', or *tate-tsuki*.

Use vertical punch as you would a normal punch. It is particularly useful for attacking the face (fig. 338).

Note the following points:

(a) Angle the fist slightly, so the knuckles of the index and middle finger make contact.

(b) Lock the thumb over the first two fingers.

(c) Tighten the fist strongly on impact.

339

340

341

342

Elbow strikes

The elbow is a powerful short range weapon. The Japanese name for it is *hiji*, though it is also known as *empi* in other styles of karate. Karate techniques use only the tip of the elbow – the forearm plays no part. Don't worry about hitting your funny-bone, because the way we use the elbow, you are unlikely to catch it.

(a) Elbow strike to mid-section   The elbow travels horizontally in this technique (fig. 339). Get into hourglass stance and bring your right arm forwards. Fully flex your elbow, so the fist is close to your chest (fig. 340). On the command, twist your hips and pull back your right elbow. Use this action to swing your left elbow upwards and forwards (fig. 341). Continue shoulder action until the left elbow is presented (fig. 342).

Note the following points:

(a) The elbow must be fully flexed, so contact does not involve the forearm.

(b) The hips and shoulders must rotate, so as to present the point of the elbow.

(c) The technique must finish sharply as the non-striking arm is brought to a stop.

The Japanese name for this technique is *hiji-ate chudan*

(b) Elbow strike to head   This technique is performed in the same way as the previous one, except that its target is the face (fig. 343). Its Japanese name is *hiji-ate jodan*.

(c) Rising elbow strike to breastbone   This strike makes use of an upwards, rather than a horizontal swing to the opponent's breastbone (fig. 344). Pull back your other elbow as the strike is made.

Note the following points:

(a) The striking action comes from the shoulder joint. The elbow must rise freely all the way to the target.

(b) The non-striking arm is pulled back with equal speed.

(d) When used from forward stance, the striking elbow lies immediately above the leading knee, and not to the side of it.

The Japanese name for this technique is *age hiji-ate*.

(d) Elbow strike to the jaw   The Japanese name for this technique is *ago hiji-ate*. Like the preceding technique, this is a rising strike, but this time the target is the jaw (fig. 345). The elbow is fully flexed and swings smoothly up in an arc (figs. 346 and 347).

343

344

345

346

347

348

349

353

Kick to mid-section, punch (or reverse punch) to head
These two techniques are known in Japanese as *kette jodan-tsuki* and *kette gyaku-tsuki jodan*. They are very similar to the techniques given on page 73–4, except that the punches are made to the head.

Practise them from forward stance, performing a front kick whilst holding one arm extended. Punch with the other arm upon landing.

BLOCKS

Knife-hand, head block
The Japanese name for this technique is *shuto jodan-uke*. It is used in the same way as a normal head block (page 51), except that the fist is replaced by knife hand (figs. 348, 349 and 350).

Ridge-hand block

The Japanese term for ridge-hand is *haito*. Ridge-hand contacts with the edge of the palm, but unlike knife-hand, it uses the thumb edge (fig. 351). The fingers are extended and the thumb flexed across the palm. Ridge-hand is effective as a groin attack (fig. 352), or as a circular strike to the face (fig. 353). Even if blocked, the strike can curl round, so the fingertips graze the opponent's eyes (fig. 354).

Ridge-hand block (*haito uchi uke*) is practised from hourglass stance by extending the left arm, with the elbow flexed and the fingers extended. The palm is turned upwards. The other arm is pulled back to the side (fig. 355). Flex your right elbow and bring the forearm across your chest with the palm turned towards the floor (fig. 356). Strongly pull back your left arm as your right moves up and outwards with a circling motion. Just as the block is about to make contact, rotate your hand palm upwards (fig. 357).

50

351

352

354

355

356

357

360

KICKS

Roundhouse kick to the head with the instep
This is perhaps the most common of the head kicks (fig. 358). Obviously it requires good hip flexibility and coordination, both of which come only after a period of regular training.

The kick is performed in the same way as the mid-section equivalent (page 86). Bring your rear leg diagonally upwards and swivel on your supporting leg (fig. 359). Point your toes and flex the knee of your kicking leg. When the knee is pointing at the target, drive out the lower leg (fig. 360).

Note the following points:

(a) The whole kicking action must be smooth and without jerkiness.

(b) The kicking knee must achieve sufficient height.

(c) The knee of the kicking leg must be flexed – many novices try to kick with a leg that is almost straight.

(d) The foot must be held firmly, with toes turned down.

(e) Lean back as the knee is rising, and you will take your body out of range of a punch. Compare this with what happens when you fail to lean back (fig. 361).

(f) Keep your head back and maintain an effective guard throughout.

The Japanese name for this kick is *mawashigeri jodan haisoku*.

High inside circling kick
The Japanese name for this technique is *mawashi-uchi keage*. Striking area is the outer edge of the foot, on the little toe side.

Bring your back leg diagonally up and across the front of your body (figs. 362 and 363). Swing the kick into the target with the outer edge of the foot leading (fig. 364).

116

359

1

362

364

117

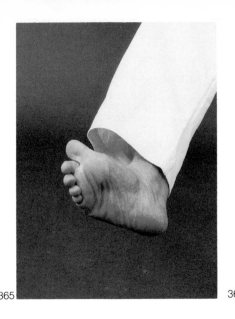
365

366

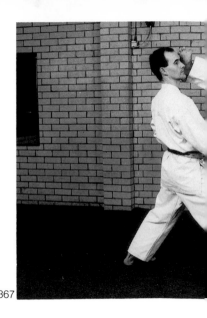
367

This technique may also be used as a block (see later).

Note the following points:

(a) The foot must rise higher than the target it is aimed at, so it is travelling slightly downwards when it makes contact.

(b) The kicking foot must be held firmly in a vertical position, so it doesn't flap about.

(c) An effective guard must be maintained at all times.

High outside circling kick

The Japanese name for this technique is *mawashi-soto keage*. It is similar to the previous technique, except that the foot travels in the reverse direction and the inside edge of the foot is used (fig. 365). This striking area is known in Japanese as *taisoku*.

Swing your back foot diagonally out (fig. 366) and upwards. The kick reaches its maximum height in front of the body (fig. 367).

SPARRING

Free-sparring (*jiu kumite*) is introduced at this point in the training programme, because now you are able to perform all the basic techniques reasonably well. If for example, you throw a front kick, you will know that the toes must be pulled back on impact. Also you have practised blocking and counter-attack sequences with a partner, so you are beginning to understand the concepts of timing and distance.

I don't intend to spend a long time discussing free sparring. It has already been well covered in my book *Winning Karate* (published by Pelham Books). Just let me say that you will be swapping fast techniques with a partner, and neither of you will know what the other is going to do until he does it!

The instructor will ask you to select a partner, so choose someone of equal size and shape. If you have protective equipment, then slip it on without delay. I recommend fist mitts and shin/instep protectors. The mitts cushion your knuckles and will protect the opponent. Shin/instep protectors take the sting out of those all-to-frequent collisions between your lower leg and the opponent's elbow.

Begin when you are told to, and not before. Work at a sensible speed and don't try to hurt your partner. Both of you are learning together, so it makes sense to cooperate. Use only techniques you know you can control, and never use excessive force. Contact to the body may be firm, but not hard enough to cause bruising. Contact to the face and head must be very light – anything more than a touch is not allowed.

Don't kick below the waist and don't attack the knees or insteps. Because of the obvious danger in using them, do not attempt open-handed attacks to the face.

Stop when you are told, and perform a standing bow to your partner before walking off.

COMBINATIONS

Front kick, side kick, reverse punch
All of these techniques are delivered to mid-section, so the Japanese description is *maegeri chudan, yoko-geri chudan, gyaku-tsuki chudan*.

Begin from fighting stance with a front kick (fig. 368). Withdraw this and set it down. Then follow with a side kick from the other leg (figs. 369 and 370). Pull the kick back to the body before setting it down and complete the combination with a reverse punch (fig. 371).

Note the following points:

(a) Collect the front kick before you set it down.

(b) Pivot on the supporting leg and lift your heel high enough to

370

371

119

deliver a correct side kick. Do not kick upwards or let the technique change into a roundhouse kick.

(c) Withdraw the side kick before setting it down and finish with a powerful punch.

One-step front kick, side kick, reverse punch
The Japanese name for this combination is *tsurikomi-maegeri chudan, yokogeri chudan, gyaku-tsuki chudan*. It is performed in the same way as the previous technique except for the opening step forwards.

Slide, snap punch to head, reverse punch to mid-section
The Japanese name for this combination is *kizami-tsuki jodan, gyaku-tsuki chudan*. Snap punch is a fast and powerful punch from the leading hand. It is useful in its own right, and it also makes a good diversion for a follow-up technique.

Begin from fighting stance by driving off your back leg. Allow the front foot to lift slightly, so it slides forward and covers ground. Before you stop moving, punch to the opponent's face with your leading hand (fig. 372) and quickly follow with a reverse punch to mid-section (fig.373). Both punches are pulled back promptly.

Note the following points:

(a) Practise the front foot slide, so it isn't telegraphed to the opponent. Novices often signal their intention by obviously shifting body weight, or lifting the front foot just before they move.

(b) Don't wait for your slide forwards to finish before you snap punch.

(c) Make the follow-up reverse punch as soon after the snap punch as possible, otherwise the opponent will see them as two separate and distinct moves. Having said that, don't blur one punch into the next.

372

373

The Blue Belt Syllabus

STANCES

Hook stance
This curious-looking stance is known as *kake-dachi* in Japanese. It is seen in some kata, often following a kick.

The leading foot is turned outwards, and the knee is well bent. The rear foot rests on the ball of the foot, with the knee pressing into the back of the leading leg (fig. 374).

Note the following points:

(a) The front foot is flat on the floor. The rear makes contact only through the ball of the foot. The heel is lifted.

(b) Both knees are well bent and the body is upright.

(c) The bottom is tucked in.

One foot forwards stance
The feet are parallel and forwards-facing. They are approximately shoulder-width apart. The heel of the leading foot is in line with the toes of the following foot, and the knees are slightly bent. The hips face forwards and the body is upright (fig. 375).

PUNCHES AND STRIKES

Augmented punch
The Japanese name for this technique is *morote-tsuki*. It is a double punch and is taught in two different ways.

Begin from hour-glass stance and draw both fists back to your hips. On the command, drive both fists forwards, so they come to a stop with thumbs either side of the centre-line of the body. Alternatively, thrust your fists out at different angles so that although they come to lie once more in the centre-line of the body, one is higher than the other.

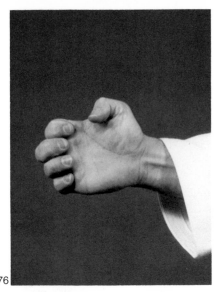

376

377

379

380

381

382

383

Note the following points:

(a) Both fists rotate from palm upwards-facing, to palm downwards-facing at the end of the first version. In the second, the lower fist remains palm upwards-facing.

(b) The fists are driven out by a shrugging action of the shoulders and come to a simultaneous stop.

Half-open fist

The Japanese name for this technique is *hiraken*. It is a form of punch in which the fingers are not folded tightly into the palm. Instead, they are folded only at the middle knuckles, and the fingertips press firmly into the pad of flesh at the base of the fingers. The thumb is locked against the side of the palm (fig. 376).

Use this technique to attack targets which are masked to a forefist (fig. 377).

Descending elbow strike

This is an effective strike which uses the weight of the descending arm to give it more power (fig. 378). Its Japanese name is *oroshi hiji-ate*.

Extend your left arm out from your body and flex the elbow through ninety degrees. Upper arm and forearm must be parallel to the ground. Turn your palm so it faces downwards. Flex your right arm too, so the fist is raised behind your head (fig. 379).

Extend your right arm fully (fig. 380), and then bring it forward and down, in front of your chest (fig. 381).

Note the following points:

(a) The fist of the striking arm must be tightly clenched on impact.

(b) Unless it is grasping hold of the opponent, the other arm is swiftly withdrawn to the hip.

(c) The body must not lean forwards as the elbow descends.

BLOCKS

Until now, we have looked at different types of blocks all of which used the arms. In this part of the training programme, we will examine ways of using the legs to block attacks.

Pressing blocks

These blocks push an attack off course, or prevent it from developing. In the first example, the ball of the foot is used in an upwards-swinging kick to drive the attacking arm upwards (fig. 382). In the second example, the edge of the foot is driven downwards onto the attacker's kick (fig. 383). This prevents his knee from rising sufficiently to deliver a kick.

384

385

Sweeping blocks

High inside circling kick (*mawashi-uchi keage*) is an effective block, sweeping the attacker's arm to one side (fig. 384). High outside circling kick (*mawashi-soto keage*) can be used in a similar manner (fig. 385).

Both rely on the blocking foot being held vertically.

Barring block

This block is effective against kicks. As the attacker launches a kick, withdraw your weight over your back leg and lift your front knee high. If you move slightly into the kick, the opponent's shin or foot will bang hard into your knee (fig. 386). Maintain an effective guard as you block.

Use this block carefully when training with a partner because it can cause painful bruising to his ankle and foot.

KICKS

Side kick to head

The Japanese name for side kick to the head is *yoko-geri jodan* (fig. 387). A great deal of hip flexibility is needed to raise the kicking leg high enough, and if this is lacking, the heel swings up in a curve rather than driving directly to the face.

The upper body leans well back and the hips rotate away from the kick.

Note the following points:

(a) The kicking knee must be raised to the correct height.

(b) The upper body must lean away to help give a direct thrust to the kick. The head is lifted.

388

(c) The supporting leg must be free to rotate and the kick makes contact with the heel and edge of the foot – not with the sole.

(d) Keep your eyes on the opponent and maintain a guard.

Roundhouse kick to head using ball of foot
This kick is similar to the one we practised in the previous section on page 116. The difference is that this kick uses the ball of the foot (fig. 388), rather than the instep.

Raise the kicking knee high as you swivel on the supporting leg. Lean well back and maintain your guard. The kick has to travel horizontally into its target, not swing upwards through a diagonal path. The latter fault makes you likely to catch your toes on elbows, or shoulders.

The foot then thrusts into the target.

391

Back kick to mid-section
The Japanese name for this technique is *ushiro-geri chudan*. It uses the heel of the foot to make contact but unlike side kick, the foot is vertical and your knee faces towards the floor (fig. 389). Your back is turned to the opponent (fig. 390), so use this kick only when it is safe to do so.

Begin from forward stance with your elbows held close to your sides. Step across with your front foot (figs. 391 and 392). Swivel around so your back is towards the opponent (fig. 393), lift your kicking leg (fig. 394), and thrust your kick back in a straight line to the target (figs. 395 and 396).

Pull the kicking leg back strongly, so the knee withdraws to your chest. At the same time, continue swivelling until you come to face the front once more.

Note the following points:

(a) Step across with your leading foot by the correct amount. If you

395

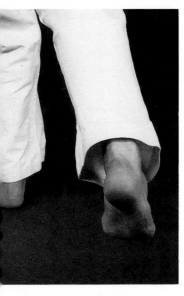

390

393

394

step too little, or too far, your kick will be off-centre. Practise until you learn how far to step.

(b) Swivel your hips smartly and turn so your back is facing directly to the rear. If you don't swivel enough, your kick will be off-centre.

(c) Keep your arms by your sides throughout the kick. Lean forward but lift your head up.

(d) Thrust kick with the heel, don't let the ball of the foot lead, and don't let the foot turn to the side.

(e) Put the kicking foot down carefully after use – don't fall forwards onto it.

As you become better at performing back kick, you will find that the

397 398

step across-swivel-kick movement smoothes out into a continuous flow of movement. It is only when you have reached this stage that you can use back kick in a sparring situation.

Experienced karateka miss out the step across-swivel movement altogether. They simply lift the rear leg and take it across the back of the supporting leg (fig. 397). The latter swivels as the kicking foot moves past (fig. 398).

It's worth repeating that when using back kick, you are in danger of being hit in the back! Therefore set your range correctly and then mask the kick with a feint, such as an attempted foot sweep.

Jumping front kick
The Japanese name for this technique is *tobi maegeri*. It is referred to as a 'jumping kick' because when it makes contact, the supporting leg is clear of the floor.

Begin from cat stance, and jump high into the air. Bring both knees up (fig. 399) and snap kick into a bag with the ball of your foot (fig. 400).

Note the following points:

(a) Jumping front kick must be delivered *when both feet are off the floor*.

(b) Lift both knees high, not just the kicking knee. Keep your elbows to your side.

(c) Kick hard into the punch bag.

(d) Collect your stance upon landing.

FREE FIGHTING

By now, you should be demonstrating that you can not only use many different techniques effectively, but you also understand

400

tactics. This is the ability to out-guess your opponent and it comes only after years of regular practice.

You see, free sparring is rather like a game of snooker in that it is not enough to pot a ball; you must also line up the next shot. If I use a front kick, I will arrange my landing so as to give me a second chance to score with a follow-up technique. At the same time I will be on my guard for the opponent's response.

Deciding what tactics to use will depend upon your opponent, so during the opening minutes of sparring, you should look out for clues which tell you how he will react. Does he shy away when you make as though to advance quickly? Or does he dig his heels in and prepare to punch? Is his stance too high, too narrow, or too long? Does his guard cover the whole of his body? Or are there gaps?

No amount of words can make up for practical experience, especially in the case of free sparring. So get out there and practise!

COMBINATIONS

Front kick to mid-section, roundhouse kick to head, reverse punch to mid-section.

The Japanese name for this sequence is *maegeri chudan, mawashigeri jodan, gyaku-tsuki chudan*. It is a straightforward sequence from a front kick, into a high roundhouse kick which rotates the hips. The kick is withdrawn and the hips straightened, before reverse punch is used.

Note the following points:

(a) Each technique must be completed before the next begins, but having said that, the whole sequence must run smoothly

(b) The final reverse punch must use strong hip twist. The punch is then pulled back sharply.

One-step front kick to mid-section, roundhouse kick to the head, mid-section reverse punch.

Except for the initial step, this technique is very similar to the preceding one. Use the step as an accelerator, varying its length to suit the situation.

One-step punch to head, reverse punch to mid-section, one step front-kick to mid-section, roundhouse kick to mid-section, and reverse punch to mid-section

This complicated sequence opens with a fast step forwards, followed by a face punch with the leading fist. As this is withdrawn, perform reverse punch to mid-section. Pull back the reverse punch and synchronise this action with a second step forwards, followed by front kick to mid-section. Move smoothly through into a roundhouse kick and finish with a strong reverse punch. The last two techniques are aimed at the opponent's mid-section.

Note the following points:

(a) The first two punches follow in quick succession. As one fist is going out, the other is being pulled back. However, each technique must be properly shown.

(b) Keep your guard in place as you step forward to front kick and withdraw it before setting your foot down. Continue through with the roundhouse kick.

(c) Turn your hips into the reverse punch, and withdraw the punching arm sharply afterwards.

The Brown Belt Syllabus

There are no new stances to learn in this section, so we can go directly on to the rest of the programme.

One-knuckle punch

The Japanese name for this technique is *ippon-ken*. There are various types of one-knuckle fist but the most common makes contact with the middle knuckle of the middle finger (fig. 401).

Roll your fingers into your palm, as though to make a normal front fist. Leave the middle finger partly extended, and jam it out by closing the index and fourth fingers. Lock the whole thing with your thumb (figs. 402 and 403).

One-knuckle punch makes contact over a small area and so it can be very effective. Having said that, it isn't well suited to hard contact on bony surfaces. Use it against the temples or the eyes.

A second type of one-knuckle fist uses the thumb. It is called

402

403

404

405

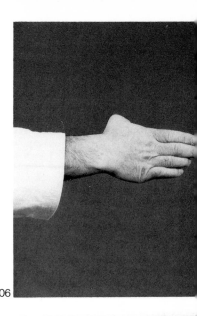

406

407

409

408

oyayubi-ken in Japanese. Make a normal fist, but press your thumb into the side of the fingers, instead of locking it underneath them as in a regular front fist (fig. 404).

Use this protruding thumb knuckle in a circular strike, hooking it around and into vulnerable targets such as the temple (fig. 405).

Back-hand strike
Back-hand strike uses the back of the open hand in a swinging strike. Extend the fingers as though for a spear-, or knife-hand, and lock the thumb across the palm (fig. 406). Flex the wrist as you strike (fig. 407) and extend the hand rapidly on impact (fig. 408).

The Japanese name for this technique is *haishu*.

Strikes using the wrist
The back of the wrist can be used either as a strike (fig. 409) or as a block (fig. 410). Flex your wrist and bring the fingers together.

411

412

413

The Japanese term for the strike is *koken-uchi*, and for the block, it is *koken-uke*.

The hand weapon known as 'chicken's beak' (*keiko*) is made by bringing the fingers and thumb together. Although a traditional karate technique, chicken's beak is hardly ever seen in modern training halls.

BLOCKS

Double circular knife block
The Japanese name for this circular block using both hands is *mawashi shuto-uke*.

Stand in hour-glass stance and extend your right arm. Bend the arm so the right hand is turned palm-up at shoulder height. The left arm is brought across the chest and rotated palm-downwards (fig. 411). Begin moving the right hand in a circle, so it passes behind the left (fig. 412). As the left hand circles upwards, the right curves downwards (fig. 413). The left hand continues to circle downwards as the right rises (fig. 414). Both palms face forwards at this point.

417

Pull both hands back to the hips, still with the palms facing forwards (fig. 415), then thrust both arms out straight, one above the other (fig. 416).

Try the following application. Your partner attacks with a punch to the face. You catch it on your left palm-edge. Immediately, the opponent punches with his other fist, only to have this blocked with your right hand (fig. 417). Continue the block and you will trap his arms (fig. 418). Then thrust him away (fig. 419).

Reverse lower parry
This is similar to the lower parry we studied on page 99. Reverse lower parry blocks with the rear hand whilst the face is guarded with the leading hand (fig. 420).

415

416

420

421

422

423

Begin from left fighting stance and as the opponent throws a front kick, drive diagonally forwards and block with your rear guarding hand (fig. 421). Turn your hips and punch him in the back of the head as he lands (fig. 422). Follow with reverse punch to mid-section (fig. 423).

The Japanese name for this technique is *gyaku-gedan barai*.

KICKS

Jumping double kick

The Japanese name for this technique is *tobi nidan-geri*. It is similar to the jumping front kick we studied on page 128, but this time, two kicks must be delivered whilst you are still in the air.

Jump up and forwards into a punch bag. Bring your left knee up high and kick hard into the bag (fig. 424). Immediately deliver a second kick whilst you are still airborne (figs. 425 and 426).

Note the following points:

(a) Jump high and kick quickly. Don't wait until you reach maximum height before throwing the first kick.

(b) Kick hard into the bag and tuck your legs beneath you.

(c) Keep your arms under control – don't let them flap about.

This kick needs a lot of explosive power in the muscles of the upper thigh. To get maximum power on take off, quickly bob down before you spring upwards.

Front stamping kick to the knee
This kick uses the heel to attack the opponent's knee joint. Bring

424

426

427

428

429

430

your kicking leg forwards and bend the knee (fig. 427). Kick upwards into the opponent's knee joint (fig. 428).

Note the following points:

(a) Keep an effective guard and don't lean forwards into the kick.

(b) Strike with the heel – not the sole of the foot.

The Japanese name for this kick is *mae-kakato fumikomi.*

Front-stamping kick to mid-section and head
This kick uses the heel in a thrust to the body (fig. 429) and face (fig. 430). Bring your kicking knee up tight against your body, then drive it out, using hip projection to add more power.

Descending heel kick to the head
This spectacular kick also uses the heel of the foot, but this time

138

432

433

downwards onto the opponent's head (fig. 431). It is very difficult to control, so practise it with care. For additional safety, extend your foot, so you make contact with the sole and not the heel.

Swing your kicking leg around and up, so the knee actually brushes the shoulder. Then drop it forcefully on the target. Don't flap your arms about.

Reverse roundhouse kick

This kick came late to karate practice. As far as I can tell, it came from the Korean martial art of *taekwondo*. Its Japanese name is *mawashi-ushirogeri*.

Begin from fighting stance by stepping across in front of your rear leg. Instead of slowing the rotation to a stop and thrusting out a straight kick, continue swivelling around, so your rear foot begins to lift (figs. 432 and 433).

Accelerate through the turn, allowing the almost straight kicking leg to rise in a diagonal, upwards-travelling circle (fig. 434). Pull your leg quickly back to the chest after contact has been made.

434

Note the following points:

(a) Use the body rotation as an accelerator, to get the kicking leg rising quickly.

(b) Lean forwards and keep your guard throughout.

(c) Allow your leg to extend as it reaches out.

(d) For safety's sake in the dojo, aim to contact with the sole of your foot rather than the traditional (and more dangerous) heel.

(e) Get back into a fighting stance as soon as possible.

COMBINATIONS

Front kick to mid-section, roundhouse kick, back kick and reverse punch
The Japanese name for this sequence is *maegeri chudan, mawashigeri, ushirogeri, gyaku-tsuki*. Going from front kick to roundhouse kick is not difficult (figs. 435 and 436), but the following back kick means that you must land well forwards, with your hips already turned (fig. 437). Correct your stance and perform back kick (fig. 438), followed by a reverse punch (fig. 439).

Note the following points:

(a) Do not pull your roundhouse kick back fully. Allow it to land well forwards, so your hips are already half-turned in the direction of the back kick.

(b) Turn your hips fully to ensure that the back kick is along the centre-line. Withdraw the kick by bringing the knee against your

435

436

437

140

438

439

body. Then set your foot down carefully as you turn to face forwards once more.

(c) Use your hips to throw a really strong reverse punch.

Mid-section front kick, back kick, reverse punch
Although this combination uses one less technique, it is actually more difficult because you have to start the hips turning from cold. In the previous combination, the hips were already half turned after the roundhouse kick.

Perform front kick normally and bring your foot back afterwards. Place it carefully across the front of the supporting leg and then spin around for a back kick.

Complete the sequence with reverse punch.

The Japanese name for this combination is *maegeri chudan, ushiro-geri chudan, gyaku-tsuki chudan*.

Slide forwards snap punch, mid-section reverse punch, one step front kick to mid-section, roundhouse kick to head, back kick to mid-section and reverse punch
This combination begins with a snap punch which is delivered at the end of a slide forwards. The drive forward is produced by the bent back leg, plus a slight shifting of body weight. Pull the punch back quickly, so it provides power for a strong reverse punch to mid-section.

Follow this with a one-step front kick, then a roundhouse kick to the head. Land with your hips already partially rotated, so you can go straight into back kick without hesitation. Complete the combination with a reverse punch to mid-section.

The Japanese name for this sequence is *kizami-tsuki jodan, gyaku-tsuki chudan, tsurikomi-maegeri chudan, mawashigeri jodan, ushirogeri chudan, gyaku-tsuki chudan*.

The Black Belt Syllabus

Examination for black belt is the toughest of all gradings but because you have been training systematically, under a gradually increasing work-load, by the time you are eligible to take the examination, you will be fit enough to handle it.

However, the coach is training a class of between fifteen and forty students, so the training programme he gives will be geared to an overall standard, rather than one specific to you. Therefore you may need to do some additional and specific training.

If you are not satisfied with some aspect of your fitness – perhaps your left hip is less flexible than your right – then you should do some specific training before the grading. If you find it difficult to perform a kata all the way through with sufficient intensity, then you need additional whole-body endurance training.

Are you confident that you know your kata well enough to be able to perform it without mistakes? Have you put in enough free-sparring time to be able to give a good account of yourself?

You must come to grips with all these things *before* the day of grading.

Having said all that, don't train yourself to extinction! Leave enough energy and enthusiasm to carry you through the day. I recommend leaving off all except very light training for the two days before grading. By all means keep yourself supple, but only by using gentle stretching exercises.

The black belt grading consists not so much of new techniques, though there are a few of these, as a re-examination of previous techniques. You may be asked to perform a technique taken from any one of the preceding grades, so it's not a question of learn 'em and forget 'em!

PUNCHES AND STRIKES

There is only one new technique to be learned for this grade, and that is 'hip twist snap punch'. Its Japanese name is *nagashi-tsuki jodan*, and it uses a special form of body movement to deliver a fast punch, whilst taking the body away from direct attack (fig. 440).

441

442

A Japanese teacher once explained how hip twist snap punch works by asking me to imagine a pebble jutting out of a fast-flowing stream. The water aproaches the pebble, then divides around it, before joining back up again, and continuing its flow. There is no hesitation and no slowing down. In the same way, hip twist snap punch simply moves around the opponent.

To practise this punch, stand in a relaxed posture, arms hanging by your sides and fists clenched lightly (fig. 441). Thrust with your rear leg, allowing the front to slide forwards. Notice how the front foot is turned inwards (fig. 442). The angle of the front foot indicates the eventual angle of the body.

As the slide comes to a stop, raise both arms and snap punch with the leading one. As you do this, twist your rear hip, and drag the rear foot round (fig. 443).

Withdraw the snap punch and return your rear foot to a centre position. Then lower both hands fully to your sides once more.

444

443

445

Note the following points:

(a) Both arms are raised together. One delivers the punch, the other provides a high guard.

(b) Don't turn the front foot too much, or you will finish at right angles to the attack, rather than at a shallow angle to it.

(c) As the body leans in behind the punch, weight eases on the rear foot, so it can slide easily with the hip twist. The hips turn as the punch extends and the back foot slides at the same time.

(d) Punch towards the original centre-line.

(e) The punch connects, the hips stop turning and the rear foot stops sliding all at the same time.

446

(f) Withdraw the punch smartly to a guard position, but return more slowly to the start position.

Hip twist snap punch combined with a step forwards makes an effective and fast attack. Begin from fighting stance and quickly step forwards (fig. 444). Maintain your guard as you step, but turn your front foot inwards. Use your hip as you punch (fig.445).

COMBINATIONS

Front kick, hip twist snap punch
Perform a normal front kick whilst retaining your original guard (fig. 446). If you change guard as you kick the punch will be weak. Set your foot down with the toes turned inwards (fig. 447).

Pull your guard back strongly and at the same time, drive your

punching hip forwards. This pulls your rear leg around and aligns the stance correctly (fig. 448).

Double kicks on the same leg
Kicking twice in succession with the same leg needs flexibility, co-ordination and balance. Without these, double kicks are impossible to perform correctly.

The first combination of kicks uses front kick followed by round-house kick. Go into fighting stance and perform a normal front kick (fig. 449). Keep weight over your supporting leg and withdraw the kick to a fully knee-flexed position (fig. 450). Swivel on your supporting leg and raise the kicking knee until the foot is horizontal. Then perform a roundhouse kick (fig. 451).

Withdraw the kicking leg, set it down and finish with a reverse punch (fig. 452).

448

449

450

451

Note the following points:

(a) Keep your shoulders relaxed and your guard firm throughout.

(b) Bring your kicking knee to full height and *do not* lower it between kicks.

(c) Lean back during the roundhouse kick but keep your head up. Drive your lower leg out sharply, whilst maintaining balance.

The second combination uses front kick, followed by side kick. Perform front kick (fig. 453) and as you pull it back, swivel your hips so your heel faces the target (fig. 454). Thrust your heel out straight (fig. 455).

Finish the sequence with a back-fist strike as you land (fig. 456), followed by a reverse punch (fig. 457).

454

455

456

457

458

148

460

461

Note the following points:

(a) The front kick must be withdrawn sharply and the hips turned fully away.

(b) The kicking leg must not drop between kicks, otherwise side kick will lose its form.

The third and final combination uses front kick followed by reverse-roundhouse kick. Perform a normal front kick (fig. 458) and withdraw your leg whilst twisting your hips. At first glance, this action seems similar to the previous sequence. However, the foot is not lifted so high (fig. 459).

Bring your foot upwards and swing it back in an arc (fig. 460). Collect it after contact by withdrawing the knee to your chest, then set the foot down and finish off with a reverse punch (fig. 461).

Note the following points:

(a) Turn your hips sharply away after the front kick.

(b) Lean your upper body back to balance the weight of the kicking leg.

(c) Pull the kick right back before setting it down.

Additional Training

BAG WORK

There are some schools of karate in which students never get to test their punches and kicks. This is not a good thing, because it leads to incorrect technique development.

It is important for karateka to test that they have:

—formed a correct fist that can withstand heavy contact without flexing painfully at the wrist, or hurting the finger joints;

—formed their foot correctly, so they strike effectively with the correct part;

—set up their stance correctly, so they don't fall over as a result of recoil;

—delivered the technique so it actually digs into the target and not just glances off the surface.

A punching bag is ideal for this purpose. Most karate techniques can be applied to the bag (fig. 462), but begin with light impacts

462

463

464

before increasing to full force. Some bags are quite heavy! You should be able to hit the bag repeatedly with full force, without jarring your joints or bruising the contact areas. However, if you are going to train for an extended period, buy yourself a pair of light bag-work gloves.

Perform techniques correctly – don't just 'slug' the bag. If the bag starts swinging wildly, ask someone to hold it for you (figs. 463, 464 and 465). As a matter of fact, correct impacts on the bag don't set it swinging. Instead they cause the bag to kink.

Target Mitts

Target mitts consist of gloves faced with thick padding. They are excellent for speed and accuracy training. Use two mitts and work

466

467

468

469

470

471

with a partner. At first, your partner simply holds the mitts whilst you run through your syllabus of techniques against them. Do note though that mitts shouldn't be used with forceful techniques such as front kick, side kick, or back kick. Use control when striking at target mitts and save heavy contact for bag-work!

Target mitts are excellent for developing reaction times, speed and accuracy.

Your partner slips the mitts over his fists and takes up a fighting stance, holding the mitts at various heights and in different directions. Turn them face-on for direct attacks such as snap punch (fig. 466), or reverse punch (fig. 467). Turn them sideways-on for back fist (fig. 468), roundhouse kick (figs. 469 and 470), or reverse-roundhouse kick (fig. 471).

The pads are moved up and down, and from side to side. Hold them apart, to encourage your partner to attack widely separated targets in quick succession.

Once you get the hang of it, attack both pads with combination techniques. If one pad faces you and the other is side-on, then hit the first pad with reverse punch (fig. 467) and the second with roundhouse kick (fig. 469). This isn't the only option of course.

Your partner can increase the level of skill needed by moving the pads about, and changing them from facing, to side-on. He can use his fighting stance to advance towards you or retreat away. If you show an opening in your guard, he can point it out painlessly with the mitts.

Glossary

Please note that the explanations given are not literal translations of Japanese into English.

Age-uchi	Rising strike
Ago	Chin
Ago-uchi	Strike to chin
Ashi barai	Leg sweep
Budo	The way of martial arts practice
Chudan-ate	Strike to mid-section
Chudan soto-uke	Mid-section outside block
Chudan-tsuki	Punch to mid-section
Chudan uchi-uke	Mid-section inside block
Chudan uke	Mid-section block
Chusoku	Ball of foot
Dachi	Stance
Dan	Grade within black belt
Do	The way
Dojo	Place of training in the way
Empi	Elbow
Fudo-dachi	'Get-ready' stance
Fumikomi	Stamping kick
Ganmen	Face
Ganmen-uchi	Strike to face
Gedan	Groin and lower body
Gedan barai	Lower parry
Gedan-tsuki	Punch to lower body
Gedan-uke	Lower block
Geri	Kick
Goju ryu	Style of karate
Gyaku	Reverse
Gyaku-mawashigeri	Reverse roundhouse kick
Gyaku-tsuki	Reverse punch
Haisoku	Instep

Haito	Inner knife-hand
Hajime	Begin
Hanmei gamae	Half-forwards facing stance
Heiko-dachi	Parallel open stance
Heisoku-dachi	Normal stance
Hidari	Left
Hiji	Elbow
Hiji age-uchi	Rising elbow strike
Hiji chudan-ate	Elbow strike to mid-section
Hiji jodan-ate	Elbow strike to head
Hiji oroshi uchi	Descending elbow strike
Hiraken	Half-open fist
Hiza	Knee
Hiza geri	Knee kick
Hizo-uchi	Strike to spleen
Ippon-ken	One knuckle punch
Ishin ryu	Karate style founded by Ticky Donovan
Jiu dachi	Fighting stance
Jiu kumite	Free sparring
Jodan-tsuki	Punch to head
Jodan-uchi	Strike to head
Jodan-uke	Head block
Jutsu	Techniques
Kakato	Heel
Kakato-geri	Heel kick
Kake-dachi	Hooked stance
Kansetsu	Joint
Kansetsu-geri	Kick to joint
Karate	Way of the empty hand
Karategi	Karate training uniform
Kata	Patterns
Keage	High kick
Keiko	Chicken's beak
Kekomi	Thrusting
Kiai	Shout
Kibadachi	Straddle stance
Kihon	Basic techniques
Kime	Focus of power
Kin-geri	Kick to groin
Kohei	Junior student
Koken	Bent wrist
Kokutsu-dachi	Back stance
Komekami	Temple
Kote	Forearm
Kumite	Sparring
Kyokushinkai	Style of karate
Kyu	Coloured belt grade
Maegeri	Front kick
Makiwara	Striking post

Mawashigeri	Roundhouse kick
Mawashigeru chusoku	Roundhouse kick using ball of foot
Mawashigeri haisoku	Roundhouse kick using instep
Mawashi kubi-geri	Roundhouse kick to neck
Mawashi-uchi	Roundhouse strike
Mawashi-uke	Roundhouse block
Mawatte	Turn
Migi	Right
Mikazuki-geri	Crescent kick
Mokuso	Meditation
Moroashi-dachi	One foot forwards stance
Morote-uke	Augmented block
Musubi-dachi	Open toe stance
Naha-te	Old Okinawan school of karate
Nanbudo	School of karate
Nekoashi-dachi	Cat stance
Nihon nukite	Two fingered spear-hand
Nukite	Spear-hand
Oi-tsuki	Lunge punch
Oroshi-uchi	Descending strike
Oyayubi ippon-ken	Thumb-knuckle fist
Pinan	System of five basic katas
Rei	Bow
Renraku waza	Combinations
Ryu	School
Sakotsu-uchi	Strike to collarbone
Sanchin-dachi	Hour-glass stance
Sankukai	School of karate
Seiken	Forefist
Seiken ago-uchi	Forefist strike to chin
Seiza	Kneel
Sempai	Senior student
Sensei	Teacher
Shihan	Master
Shikodachi	Sumo stance
Shita-tsuki	Short punch
Shito ryu	Style of karate
Shotei	Palm heel
Shotokai	Style of karate
Shotokan	Style of karate
Shukokai	Style of karate
Shuri-te	Old Okinawan school of karate
Shuto	Knife-hand
Shuto ganmen-uchi	Knife-hand strike to face
Shuto hizo-uchi	Knife-hand strike to spleen
Shuto jodan-uke	Knife-hand head block
Shuto sakotsu-uchi	Knife-hand strike to collarbone
Shuto uke	Knife-hand block
Sokuto	Knife-edge of foot

Soto harai-uke	Outer sweeping block
Taikyoku	Simple introduction to katas
Taisoku	Inner edge of foot
Tameshiwari	Wood breaking
Tate-tsuki	Half-twisted fist
Te	Hand
Tettsui	Hammerfist
Tomari-te	Old Okinawan school of karate
Tsuruashi-dachi	Crane on a rock stance
Uchi	Strike
Uchi hachiji-dachi	Pigeon-toe stance
Uchi harai-uke	Inside sweeping block
Uke	Block
Uraken	Back-fist
Uraken hizo-uchi	Back-fist to spleen
Ushirogeri	Back kick
Wado ryu	Style of karate
Yamei	Stop
Yoi	Get ready
Yoko	Side
Yoko-geri	Side kick
Yoko keage	High side kick
Zenkutsu-dachi	Forward stance

Useful Addresses

The Ishin Ryu Karate Association has clubs in east London, south-east London, Essex, Suffolk and Norfolk. If you want to do karate and live in any of these areas, then write to:

The Ishin Ryu Karate Association
Citygate Holdings
Citygate House
399–425 Eastern Avenue
Gants Hill
London IG2 6LR
Tel: 01-505 7337

If you are interested in karate training but live outside these areas, then contact:

The Martial Arts Commission
4–16 Deptford Bridge
London SE8 4JS
Tel: 01-691 3433

Whichever address you write to, be sure to enclose a stamped addressed envelope.

Additional Reading

If you enjoyed this book, then you will appreciate *Winning Karate* by Ticky Donovan, published by Pelham Books.

The following books may also be of interest:

Official Karate by David Mitchell, published by Stanley Paul.

Karate - The Complete Course by T. Morris, published by Guinness.

Beginning Karate and *Fighting Fit*, both by David Mitchell, published by Unwin Hyman.

Karate in Action by Peter Spanton, published by Stanley Paul.